Guardians of the Exchequer

(Life Inside the Indian Revenue Service (IRS)

AF866632

Thakur Shailendra Nath

PG PUBLICATIONS

Delhi- 110089 (India)

Edition : 2026
ISBN : 978-93-6210-515-8

Price : 400/ -

Guardians of the Exchequer
(Life Inside the Indian Revenue Service (IRS)
-Thakur Shailendra Nath
Mail id : thakurshailendranath@gmail.com

Cover Page & Book Layout
Nidhi Kanojiya

Published by
PRAKHAR GOONJ PUBLICATIONS
Office : A - 11/90, Sector - 18 Rohini, Delhi - 110089
Reg. Office : H - 3/2 Sector - 18 Rohini, Delhi - 110089
Email : prakhargoonj@gmail.com
info@prakhargoonjpublications.com
Ph. : 7982710571, 7838505899, 011 - 42635077
Web : prakhargoonjpublications.com

Authors Note

I am pleased to present my latest book titled Guardians of the Exchequer - Life Inside the Indian Revenue Service(IRS) before the readers.

This book explores what it truly means to live and work inside one of India's most powerful yet least understood institutions where authority is immense, scrutiny constant, and public appreciation often scarce, but where the state itself is funded, sustained, and legitimised.

Public finance is the silent backbone of a nation. Roads, schools, hospitals, national security, and social welfare all ultimately rest upon the strength and integrity of a country's revenue system. Yet the individuals who safeguard this system often work far from public attention. This book is an attempt to shed light on their world.

The Indian Revenue Service (IRS) occupies a unique place in India's governance architecture. Tasked with administering complex tax laws and ensuring the steady flow of revenue to the national exchequer, IRS officers stand at the intersection of law, economics, public administration, and citizen engagement. Their work involves not only enforcing compliance but also maintaining fairness, building trust in the tax system, and adapting to an economy that is constantly evolving.

Guardians of the Exchequer seeks to capture the professional journey, ethical dilemmas, institutional challenges, and quiet satisfactions that accompany life in this service. Behind every assessment order, audit objection, enforcement action, or policy reform lies a human story of responsibility, resilience, and commitment to public duty.

This book does not claim to represent every experience within the IRS. Rather, it draws upon observations, conversations, and reflections from years spent within the ecosystem of tax administration. The narratives presented here aim to offer readers, students of public policy, civil servants, researchers, and citizens, a closer look at how revenue administration functions on the ground.

In an era where governance is increasingly scrutinized and expectations from public institutions continue to rise, the role of tax administrators becomes even more critical. The credibility of the tax system depends not only on laws and technology but also on the integrity, professionalism, and judgment of those entrusted to implement them.

I am thankful and obliged to writers of various books and editors of magazines and newspapers which I have consulted and taken help while writing this book. I am also thankful to the publisher who has published this book.

If this book helps readers better understand the responsibilities, pressures, and values that guide officers who serve as guardians of the nation's exchequer, it will have achieved its purpose.

Thakur Shailendra Nath
Thane

Contents

INTRODUCTION

The taxation policy of ancient India, particularly under Chanakya, combined economic rationality, ethical restraint, and administrative rigour. Far from being primitive, it reflected a sophisticated understanding of fiscal policy, balancing state needs with taxpayer welfare, a lesson of enduring relevance for modern public finance.

The taxation system of ancient India was guided by the principles of dharma (justice), welfare of subjects, and sustainability of the state. Taxes were seen not merely as revenue instruments but as a social contract between the ruler and the people.

General Features of Ancient Indian Taxation

Moderation and equity were central. Excessive taxation was condemned as unjust and destabilizing.Taxes were usually a share of production, not arbitrary levies.

The king was entitled to revenue only in return for protection and good governance.

Tax collection was adapted to local conditions, seasons, and calamities.Finding specific mentions of "indirect tax" in ancient Sanskrit texts requires looking at the principles of Rajadharma (the duty of kings) and Arthashastra (economics). While the modern term "indirect tax" didn't exist, ancient scholars described taxes on trade, imports, and sales (tolls and duties) that function exactly like modern indirect taxes.

1. The Principle of Moderation (The Bee Metaphor)

The most famous philosophy of taxation in Sanskrit comes from the Mahabharata and the Manusmriti. It suggests that a King should collect taxes (including trade duties) without hurting the source, much like a bee collects nectar.

यथा फलेन युज्येत राजा कर्ता च कर्मणाम्।
तथा वेक्ष्ये नृपो राष्ट्रे कल्पयेत्सततं करान्॥

(Manusmriti 7.128)

- **Transliteration:**

  Yathā phalena yujyeta rājā kartā ca karmaṇām |

  Tathā veksye nṛpo rāṣṭre kalpayetsatataṃ karān ||

- **Meaning:**

The King should arrange the taxes in his kingdom in such a manner that both the King and the businessman (the doer of the work) receive a fair profit/result.

2. Taxes on Trade and Commerce (Shulka)

In ancient India, indirect tax was referred to as Shulka (customs/tolls). This shloka explains that taxes should be levied after considering the costs incurred by the merchant.

क्रयविक्रयमध्वानं भक्तं च सपरिव्ययम्।
योगक्षेमं च सम्प्रेक्ष्य वणिजो दापयेत्करान्॥

(Manusmriti 7.127)

- **Transliteration:**

  Krayavikrayamadhvānaṃ bhaktaṃ ca saparivyayam|

  Yogakṣemaṃ ca samprekṣya vaṇijo dāpayetkarān ||

- **Meaning:**

After considering the purchase and sale price, the distance traveled, the cost of food and condiments, and the charges for securing the goods (insurance/security), the King shall make the merchants pay the tax.

3. Gradual Collection

The Mahabharata (Shanti Parva) emphasizes that taxing trade should be gradual so as not to discourage the trader.

अल्पाल्पेनादनीयेन वार्याद्यैः कुरुते क्षयम्।
तथा राजापि राष्ट्रेभ्यः कल्पयेत् फलमात्मनः॥

- **Transliteration:**

  Alpālpenādanīyena vāryādyaiḥ kurute kṣayam |

  Tathā rājāpi rāṣṭrebhyaḥ kalpayet phalamātmanaḥ ||

- **Meaning:**

  Just as a person draws water from a well little by little, or as a leech draws blood without the host feeling much pain, the King should extract taxes from his kingdom gradually.

In the context of indirect taxes (GST, Customs, etc.), these shlokas highlight three timeless principles:

- **Neutrality:** The tax shouldn't be so high that it kills the business.
- **Net Profit Taxation:** Taxes should be levied after accounting for the merchant's expenses (similar to the "Input Tax Credit" logic).
- **Sustainability:** The state grows only when the taxpayers (merchants and consumers) grow.

The Vedic Period (c. 1500 – 600 BCE)

In the early Vedic period, taxation was informal. As society was tribal, the "tax" was largely voluntary.

- **Bali:** Originally a voluntary offering of grain or livestock made by the people to the King (Rajan) to seek protection.
- **Evolution:** By the later Vedic period, Bali became

mandatory as the King's role shifted from a tribal leader to a territorial ruler.

The Laws of Manu (Manusmriti)

The Manusmriti (compiled between 200 BCE – 200 CE) provided the legal and moral framework for taxation. It emphasized fairness based on the nature of the trade:

- **Agriculture:** 1/6th, 1/8th, or 1/12th of the produce (depending on soil fertility).
- **Gold and Cattle:** 1/50th of the profit or increase in stock.
- **Artisans:** Usually one day of free labor per month.
- **Exemptions:** Sages, students (Brahmacharis), and the destitute were often exempt from paying taxes.

Chanakya's Taxation Philosophy

Chanakya, the chief architect of the Mauryan state (4th century BCE), provided the most systematic exposition of taxation in his treatise, the Arthashastra.

1. **Principle of Ability and Productivity**

- Taxes were linked to capacity to pay.
- Agricultural tax (bhāga) generally ranged from one-sixth to one-fourth of produce, depending on fertility and irrigation.
- Artisans, traders, and professionals were taxed according to income and turnover.

2. **Sources of Revenue**

Chanakya identified multiple streams of state revenue:

- Land revenue (primary source)
- Customs duties on trade and transit
- Excise on goods like liquor and salt

- Mining and forest produce
- State monopolies (metals, arms, liquor)
- Fines and penalties

3. **Welfare-Oriented Taxation**

- Tax relief during famine, floods, or war was mandated.
- New settlements and reclaimed lands enjoyed temporary tax exemptions.
- The king was warned that over-taxation would destroy economic activity, likened to "milking a cow without hurting it."

4. **Administrative Vigilance**

- Emphasis on efficient collection and prevention of corruption.
- Strict audits of tax officials.
- Severe punishment for embezzlement, reflecting Chanakya's realism about human nature.

5. **Moral and Political Limits**

- Chanakya explicitly cautioned that oppressive taxation leads to rebellion.
- The ruler's legitimacy depended on fair taxation and public trust.
- Revenue was to be spent on defence, administration, public works, and relief.

Tax on the Rich

Merely attaching a tax to a luxury item does not guarantee that the burden of taxation will fall on those who can most easily afford it. The enduring question in public finance therefore remains: who really bears the burden of taxation?

History offers many instructive and often ironic answers. One of the most curious attempts to tax the rich unfolded far from the usual centres of power, on the Queen Emma Bridge across St Anna Bay in Curaçao, in the former Netherlands Antilles. Between 1901 and 1934, a toll of two cents (NAf) was imposed on those crossing the bridge but only on people wearing shoes. The intent was progressive: to spare the poor while taxing those presumed affluent.

The outcome, however, defied logic. Many poor residents, unwilling to admit their poverty, borrowed shoes so they could cross the bridge "respectably" and dutifully paid the toll. Meanwhile, several wealthy Curaçaoans, unwilling to part with even a trivial sum, crossed barefoot and avoided the tax altogether. Pride and parsimony, it turned out, defeated fiscal idealism.

A similar pattern emerges when one surveys eighteenth-century Britain's tax experiments. Policymakers there identified hats as a promising tax base for two reasons. First, the wealthy often owned several expensive cocked hats, while the poor owned at most one cheap hat or none at all. Second, hats were conspicuous; unlike income, they were easy to observe.

Accordingly, in 1784 the British government introduced the Hat Tax, requiring each hat to carry a revenue stamp pasted inside its lining. The duty varied according to the hat's price, and penalties for evasion were severe. Those who failed to pay faced heavy fines, while forgers of revenue stamps could even be sentenced to death.

Predictably, resistance followed innovation. To avoid taxation, milliners simply stopped calling their creations "hats". This forced the government into the absurd task of repeatedly redefining "headgear" to keep pace with fashion. Wigs, equally visible, difficult to conceal, and associated with prosperity soon attracted the taxman's attention as well (along with an inevitable host of lice). In 1795, Britain imposed an annual one-guinea tax on the right to use the scented powders applied to wigs to mask odour. Since pigtails remained fashionable, taxpayers subject to this levy acquired the enduring nickname "guinea pigs."

These episodes underline a fundamental truth: consumption patterns do not reliably indicate affluence. Not all wealthy gentlemen owned derby horses, just as not all hat-wearers were rich. The history of taxation is, in large part, the story of people attempting to shift the burden onto someone else captured memorably in the old saying: "Don't tax you, don't tax me; tax the fellow behind the tree."

Money, after all, has neither colour nor smell. The Roman maxim pecunia non olet money does not stink originated from Emperor Vespasian's infamous urine tax in the first century CE. It serves as a reminder that states are often indifferent to the moral origins of revenue, so long as it fills the treasury. As Jean-Baptiste Colbert famously observed, the art of taxation consists in plucking the goose to obtain the largest possible number of feathers with the least possible amount of hissing.

The Indian Revenue Service: From Authority to Legitimacy

The Indian Revenue Service (IRS) is among the oldest continuously functioning administrative institutions in India. Its evolution is inseparable from the evolution of the Indian state itself. Conceived as a colonial instrument to extract resources for an empire, the service has survived independence, embraced socialism, adapted to liberalisation, and now stands transformed by digital governance.

This book examines that journey from authority to legitimacy, from coercion to consent, and from discretion to algorithms.

1. **Colonial Genesis: Revenue as the Spine of Empire (1858–1919)**

The British colonial state rested fundamentally on revenue. After the Revolt of 1857, Crown rule required a professional, centralised, and loyal fiscal machinery capable of financing administration, the military, and imperial trade.

In 1860, the Imperial Revenue Service was established, overseeing land revenue, customs, excise, and income tax. That same year, income tax was introduced in India primarily to offset wartime financial losses. Colonial revenue administration was characterised by:

- Centralisation of authority
- Minimal accountability to the population
- A compliance regime rooted in coercion

Revenue officers functioned as agents of control rather than public servants. The objective was extraction, not equity.

2. **Indianisation and Structural Consolidation (1919–1947)**

The early twentieth century witnessed:

- Expansion of income tax alongside industrial growth
- Gradual Indianisation of lower and middle ranks
- Continued British dominance in senior positions

Despite growing administrative sophistication, the revenue system remained opaque and intimidating. Taxpayers perceived it as arbitrary and hostile an institutional legacy that independent India would struggle to overcome.

3. **Post-Independence Rebirth: From Imperial to** Indian (1947–1960s)

After Independence, the Imperial Revenue Service was reconstituted as the Indian Revenue Service, operating under the authority of the Constitution of India. Key reforms included:

- Recruitment through the UPSC and through departmental promotion.
- Alignment with constitutional values
- Revenue mobilisation for nation-building and welfare

The service was bifurcated into:

- IRS (Income Tax) – direct taxes
- IRS (Customs & Central Excise) – indirect taxes

The IRS ceased to be an arm of the empire and became an instrument of planned development.The Indian Revenue Service (IRS), comprising the Income Tax and Customs & Indirect Taxes cadres, is primarily a Group 'A' Central Civil Service.

While direct recruitment through the Civil Services Examination (CSE) conducted by the UPSC remains the principal mode of induction, a significant and institutionally important channel is departmental promotion from Group 'B' feeder services. This route ensures continuity, institutional memory, and recognition of long-standing service.Departmental promotion to the Indian Revenue Service is not merely a personnel process; it is a recognition of institutional loyalty and experiential competence. While the system suffers from procedural delays and inter-cadre tensions, it remains an essential pillar of administrative balance. A transparent, time-bound, and litigation-free promotion mechanism is crucial for maintaining morale and effectiveness within India's revenue administration.

Feeder Cadres for Departmental Promotion

Departmental promotions to the IRS are made from Group 'B' Gazetted Officers of the respective departments:

Income Tax Department

Income Tax Officers (ITO – Group 'B' Gazetted). These officers typically have 15–20 years of service, including time spent in non-gazetted positions before promotion to Group.

After selection, successful candidates undergo a 3-month Foundation Course at the Lal Bahadur Shastri National Academy of Administration (LBSNAA) in Mussoorie, Uttarakhand, and NACIN Faridabad.

National Academy of Customs, Indirect Taxes, and Narcotics

This involves very dynamic training in specialised matters of conventional tax administration be it direct or indirect–along with unarmed combat, weapons, and explosives. Additionally, IRS officers undergo extensive training with the Army and the National Police Academy, and many other prestigious institutes of the country so that they are better prepared to excel in their multifaceted role. NADT and NACIN both have signed a memorandum of understanding with the National Law School of India University in Bengaluru to award postgraduate diplomas in business laws to the officer trainees. Recently, the Finance Ministry has approved the exchange of officer trainees to various countries across the world such as the Netherlands, Belgium, Switzerland, France, Australia, Malaysia, United States of America, Brazil, South Africa and OECD Nations, for increasing exposure to the future administrators.

NACIN, the National Academy of Customs, Indirect Taxes and Narcotics is the apex training and capacity-building institution for officers working under CBIC, including those in GST administration. Its importance for GST officers is both foundational and continuous.

At the entry stage, NACIN shapes how an officer understands the law. GST is not just about sections and notifications; it involves interpretation, technology platforms, audit methods, investigation standards, and taxpayer interface. NACIN's induction programmes build this base so officers start with uniform knowledge, common procedures, and a shared administrative culture across India.

As officers move ahead in service, the Academy becomes the backbone of mid-career learning. GST law evolves rapidly through Council decisions, court rulings, circulars, and system changes in GSTN. NACIN regularly updates officers through refresher courses, thematic workshops, and e-learning modules so field formations remain aligned with current legal and procedural positions.

Another critical role is specialisation. Modern GST administration needs skills in audit, anti-evasion, data analytics, intelligence, refunds, legal drafting, and adjudication. NACIN develops domain expertise in these areas and trains officers to handle increasingly complex business structures and fraud patterns.

NACIN also acts as a bridge between policy and implementation. When new schemes or amendments are introduced, master trainers are prepared who then disseminate learning across zones, ensuring consistency in practice and reducing interpretational disputes.

Equally important is its emphasis on soft skills and ethics, communication with taxpayers, principles of natural justice, quality of orders, and use of technology. This helps create a more transparent and service-oriented tax administration.

In short, for a GST officer, NACIN is not merely a training school; it is the institution that supports professional competence throughout the career from probationer to senior leadership.

There are various mid-career training programmes (MCTP) for IRS officers to keep them abreast of the latest developments in the areas of governance, particularly taxation, finance and management. These include advanced mid-career training (AMCTP), which is conducted in 3 phases. Phase I is for joint and additional commissioners, Phase II is for commissioners and principal commissioners, and Phase III is for chief commissioners and principal chief commissioners. The AMCTP generally consists of a 3-week domestic module held at premier management institutes in the country followed by a 2-week international component at internationally acclaimed universities, depending on their areas of expertise.

NACIN today is far more than a classroom institution; it directly influences career progression, capability building, and the way GST policy gets translated into field practice. In effect, NACIN shifted from being primarily a training academy to becoming a national knowledge, standardisation, and capacity-building engine for indirect tax administration.

While promotions in CBIC are governed by recruitment rules, vigilance status, APARs, and DPC processes, NACIN plays an important supporting role.

a. Mandatory/expected training milestones

For several grades, officers are expected to complete prescribed induction or mid-career programmes. Non-completion can delay consideration or make an officer ineligible until the requirement is met.

b. Weight in performance perception

Participation in specialised or advanced courses signals professional seriousness. Officers who build expertise in audit, investigation, GST analytics, international taxation etc. are often viewed as better suited for sensitive or leadership postings.

c. Empanelment & leadership grooming

For senior ranks, NACIN runs management development and leadership programmes. These programmes expose officers to policy thinking, inter-departmental coordination, and strategic administration qualities relevant for empanelment.

d. Faculty/resource roles

Officers who serve as NACIN faculty, guest trainers, or subject experts often gain visibility at higher administrative levels, which can positively influence career opportunities.

So NACIN may not "promote" someone, but it strongly shapes how prepared and credible an officer appears when promotion or empanelment is considered.

2. Flagship courses GST officers typically attend

The mix changes with seniority, but broadly officers encounter:

Induction level

- Foundation course for direct recruits
- GST law, procedures, return scrutiny
- Basics of audit & anti-evasion
- Court procedures, drafting of notices/orders
- IT systems & GSTN modules

Executive/mid-career

- Advanced GST audit
- Intelligence & investigation techniques
- Data analytics and risk management
- Refunds & export procedures
- Adjudication and quasi-judicial functions
- Litigation management

Senior officers

- Leadership & change management
- Policy implementation workshops

- International best practices
- Trade facilitation & stakeholder engagement

Plus, NACIN now runs continuous online learning through webinars and digital modules whenever major legal or system changes occur.

3. How NACIN's role expanded after GST (vs pre-GST era)

Before GST, training was largely split between Central Excise, Service Tax, and Customs streams. The focus was more on tariff, classification, and departmental procedures.

After GST, NACIN's role widened dramatically:

a. National uniformity

GST required harmonised interpretation across the country. NACIN became central to ensuring "one law, one understanding".

b. Technology-driven administration

Officers now need skills in portal-based processes, data mining, and electronic evidence. Training moved strongly toward digital capability.

c. Faster law evolution

Frequent Council decisions mean continuous re-training. NACIN functions almost like a real-time knowledge update hub.

d. Greater taxpayer interface

With self-assessment and faceless processes, communication quality, order writing, and principles of natural justice gained prominence.

e. Collaboration with states and other agencies

NACIN increasingly hosts joint programmes, international cooperation, and cross-learning initiatives.

Specialized Course:-

To become an expert GST officer (i.e., specialize in Goods and Services Tax law, compliance, assessment, policy, and administration), the best path combines formal education, professional certification, and practical experience. There isn't just one "best" course but several strong options depending on your starting point and goals.

Here's how to think about it:

Core Areas You Need to Master

An expert GST officer should be strong in:

- Indirect Tax Law (GST, Customs, Excise, VAT)
- GST Compliance & Returns
- Audit & Assessment Procedures
- Tax Policy & Administration
- Accounting & Financial Reporting
- Legal Interpretation & Litigation

Best Courses & Qualifications

1. **Chartered Accountant (CA)**

- **Why it's excellent:** In-depth taxation, law, auditing, accounting, and GST.
- **Who it's best for:** Students after 10th/12th who want taxation as a core expertise.
- **Pros:** Highly respected, deep technical grounding.
- **Cons:** Long and rigorous; not specific to GST only, but very tax-rich.

2. **Company Secretary (CS)**

- **Why:** Strong in corporate law, compliance, indirect taxes including GST.
- **Best for:** Law + compliance oriented individuals.

- **Pros:** Excellent for advisory, compliance departments.
- **Cons:** Not as accounting-intensive as CA.

3. **Cost & Management Accountant (CMA / ICMAI)**

- **Why:** Focuses on cost, taxation, accounting, audit.
- **Pros:** Strong analytical and cost approach.
- **Cons:** Less law-focused compared to CS.

4. **LLB with Specialization in Tax Law**

- **Why:** Legal foundation + specific tax law expertise.
- **Best For:** Those who want to handle litigation, consultancy, policy interpretation.
- **Pros:** Deep understanding of statutes & appellate process.
- **Cons:** Requires extra study of accounting to understand GST compliance.

5. **Specialized GST Certification Courses**

These are focused short courses designed specifically around GST.

Some recognized ones include:

- ICAI - Certificate Course on GST (for CA students & professionals)
- ICSI - GST Courses (for CS & aspiring professionals)
- NIRC of ICAI/Other Regional GST Programs
- National Academy of Customs, Indirect Taxes and Narcotics (NACIN) training programs
- Online platforms: Coursera, Udemy, edX - GST diplomas & modules

These are excellent add-ons but not enough by themselves for an expert role.

6. **Government / Civil Services Path**

If you want to become a GST officer in Govt. service (CBIC/Indirect Tax Department):

Indian Revenue Service (IRS) – Customs & Indirect Taxes

- Entry via UPSC Civil Services Exam
- Offers direct GST administration career
- Training at NACIN (GoI)
- Real specialization in GST law & procedure

Recommended Pathways by Goal

Goal: Government GST Officer

- LLB or Graduation → UPSC → IRS (Customs & Indirect Taxes)
- NACIN specialized GST training

Goal: Corporate Tax Expert / GST Consultant

- CA or CMA or CS
- Add: Certified GST Courses
- Gain experience in compliance, audits, returns

Goal: Legal Advisory/Tax Litigation

- LLB → Master's in Tax Law
- Specialized GST courses

Suggested Study Roadmap

- Build a strong foundation in accounting + law
- Learn GST Act, Rules, Returns, Assessment
- Practice real filings & audits
- Stay updated with amendments & GST Council decisions

4. **Socialist State and the Expansion of Power (1960s–1980s)**

India's socialist economic framework profoundly reshaped tax administration:

- Extremely high tax rates
- Proliferation of exemptions and controls
- Vast discretionary authority vested in officers

This period saw aggressive enforcement, frequent raids and prosecutions, and the parallel expansion of the black economy. While revenues increased, the legitimacy of tax administration suffered. Power without commensurate accountability bred corruption risks and eroded public trust.

5. Liberalisation and Administrative Reorientation (1991–2010)

Economic liberalisation in 1991 marked a turning point. The IRS was required to transform from a control-oriented body into a facilitative institution supporting growth. Reforms included:

- Reduction in tax rates
- Simplification of laws
- Introduction of PAN, TDS systems, and digitisation

The officer's role began shifting from inspector to administrator, from enforcer to regulator.

6. The Digital IRS and the Trust Deficit (2010–Present)

The last decade has witnessed unprecedented change:

- Faceless assessments and appeals
- AI-driven risk management
- GST (2017), fundamentally redefining indirect taxation

The stated objective is "trust-based tax administration." Yet challenges remain: algorithmic opacity, reduced empathy, and new questions of accountability in faceless systems. The IRS today stands at the intersection of technology, power, and public trust.

The Indian Revenue Service (IRS) occupies a unique place in the architecture of the Indian state. Tasked with mobilising resources for governance while safeguarding fairness and legality, it stands at the intersection of authority, ethics, and public trust. Like any long-standing institution exercising coercive power, the IRS carries within it moments of deep pride as well as episodes of regret. Together, they form the moral history of the service.

The Indian Revenue Service (IRS) occupies a critical position in India's fiscal architecture, yet the service today confronts a complex mix of structural, ethical, technological, and human challenges. Drawing from policy debates and lived administrative experience, there are challenges in the performance of service.The challenges of the Indian Revenue Service are not merely administrative they reflect deeper tensions between power and restraint, enforcement and trust, discretion and accountability. Sustainable reform lies not only in technology or laws, but in institutional culture: empowering officers, protecting integrity, encouraging reasoned risk-taking, and rebuilding trust with taxpayers. Only then can the IRS evolve from a revenue-collecting authority into a genuinely respected pillar of democratic governance.

The Weight of Authority

The Indian Revenue Service (IRS) stands at a paradoxical crossroads. Entrusted with the sovereign power to tax, search, seize, and prosecute, its officers exercise some of the most intrusive authority available to the State. Yet, they operate under intense scrutiny, public suspicion, political pressure, and institutional anxiety. The modern IRS is no longer merely a collector of revenue; it is an arbiter of trust between the citizen and the State. This expanded role has magnified long-standing fault lines within the service and exposed new vulnerabilities in an era of transparency, technology, and globalised finance.

In recent decades, the IRS has been tasked with responsibilities far beyond traditional tax collection. Officers are expected to combat black money, enforce anti-money laundering provisions, regulate international taxation, and contribute to economic policy enforcement. Each new statute adds another layer of expectation, often without commensurate augmentation of manpower or institutional capacity.

The result is chronic overload. Officers juggle assessments, investigations, litigation, grievance redressal, audit replies, and court appearances frequently at the cost of depth, reflection, and reasoned decision-making. Revenue targets loom large, narrowing the discretionary space required for fairness and judgment.

Indian tax administration was born in a colonial ethos of extraction rather than consent. Despite reformist rhetoric, remnants of this adversarial mindset persist. For many taxpayers, interaction with the IRS remains a source of anxiety rather than assurance.

Aggressive assessments, frequent searches, and prolonged litigation contribute to a perception of coercion. While enforcement is essential, excessive reliance on it undermines voluntary compliance, the very foundation of a modern tax system. Officers, caught between revenue expectations and taxpayer rights, often default to defensiveness rather than dialogue.

One of the most debilitating challenges within the IRS is its deep-rooted litigation culture. Appeals are often filed reflexively, even where legal issues are settled or revenue implications are marginal. The fear of audit objections and vigilance inquiries discourages officers from exercising discretion in favour of finality.

This institutional risk-aversion clogs tribunals and courts, delays revenue realisation, and damages credibility. Ironically, the system punishes officers more for alleged "loss of revenue" than for harassment or unjustified litigation, skewing incentives decisively against fairness.

High discretionary power has always been the IRS's greatest strength and its greatest vulnerability. Assessments, searches, settlements, and prosecutions require judgment, but discretion inevitably invites temptation and suspicion.

While corruption cannot be condoned, the prevailing vigilance regime often operates with the logic of presumption rather than proof. Honest officers may find themselves investigated years after retirement for decisions taken in good faith. This retrospective scrutiny fosters a culture of fear, encouraging procedural conformity over substantive justice.

Few services face the intensity of external pressure that the IRS does. High-value cases often involve politically connected individuals or powerful corporate entities. Officers may encounter informal signals, overt requests, or subtle warnings.

Transfers and postings, when perceived as opaque or punitive, become tools of discipline rather than administration. Such practices weaken institutional morale and erode the service's capacity to act independently and professionally.

Technology and the Faceless Experiment

The introduction of faceless assessment and appeals marked a radical attempt to reduce discretion and human interface. In principle, it promised objectivity and transparency. In practice, the transition has been uneven.

Officers struggle with rigid timelines, system limitations, and algorithmic risk parameters that may not capture commercial realities. Taxpayers, on the other hand, experience depersonalised processes where explanation gives way to templated communication. Technology, rather than becoming an enabler, sometimes becomes a new layer of opacity.

Human Cost Behind the Files

Behind the files and figures lie human lives. IRS officers work under relentless pressure, with long hours, frequent transfers, and constant public scrutiny. Career stagnation, limited opportunities for specialisation, and lack of structured mental health support take a silent toll.

Families absorb the costs, disrupted schooling, social isolation, and the strain of living under vigilance's long shadow. Yet, institutional discourse rarely acknowledges these personal sacrifices.

The advent of GST transformed indirect taxation but introduced new coordination challenges. September 2025 GST reforms introduced a two slab structure and a simplified governance. Consumer sentiment has soared, with festive sales reaching rupees 6lakh crore. Importantly these moves are not revenue losses as a resultant consumption and growth spurt will increase tax collections in coming years. IRS officers must now operate within a shared federal framework alongside state tax administrations with varying capacities and cultures.

Jurisdictional disputes, overlapping investigations, and information asymmetries complicate enforcement. Revenue volatility adds pressure to "perform," sometimes at the expense of cooperative federalism.

Perhaps the most profound challenge facing the IRS is one of legitimacy. Raids televised as spectacles, selective leaks to the media, and public judgments before adjudication erode trust. The officer becomes either a villain or a weapon, rarely a neutral administrator.

In a democracy, tax administration must command

respect, not fear. Rebuilding that respect requires restraint, transparency, and empathy qualities that institutional incentives do not always reward.

The challenges of the Indian Revenue Service are symptomatic of a deeper institutional dilemma: how to wield power without becoming captive to it. Reform cannot be limited to technology upgrades or legislative amendments. It must address culture how officers are trained, protected, evaluated, and trusted.

A mature IRS must encourage reasoned risk-taking, protect integrity, reduce fear-driven litigation, and reimagine its relationship with taxpayers. Only then can it evolve from an instrument of enforcement into a pillar of democratic governance strong in authority, but stronger in legitimacy.

As of late 2025, the "common citizen verdict" on the Goods and Services Tax (GST) in India has shifted from early skepticism to a more positive, though nuanced, acceptance. This change is largely driven by the major "GST 2.0" reforms implemented in September 2025, which significantly simplified the tax structure.

The current sentiment can be broken down into the following key areas:

1. **The "GST 2.0" Relief (September 2025)**

The biggest shift in public opinion occurred after the government collapsed the complex multi-slab system into a primarily two-slab structure (5% and 18%).

- **Essential Items:** Taxes on daily household essentials (soaps, toothpaste, hair oil) were slashed from 18% to 5%, leading to a visible reduction in monthly grocery bills for the middle class.
- **Insurance & Healthcare:** A major win for citizens was the removal of GST on life and health insurance premiums, which had been a long-standing demand to make social security more affordable.

- **Middle-Class "Luxuries":** Items previously in the 28% "luxury" bracket, like two-wheelers, entry-level ACs, and cement, were moved to 18%, making home ownership and personal mobility more accessible.

2. **Benefits Acknowledged by Citizens**

Most citizens now recognize several structural improvements over the old regime:

- **Price Transparency:** Unlike the pre-2017 era where taxes were hidden at every stage (tax-on-tax), GST is visible on the final bill, giving consumers a clearer idea of what they are paying to the government.
- **National Uniformity:** The "One Nation, One Tax" concept has stabilized prices across state borders, eliminating the "border-entry" price hikes that used to vary by state.
- **Digital Convenience:** For small entrepreneurs and freelancers (who make up a large part of the "common man" workforce), the fully digital filing system has reduced the need for frequent physical visits to tax offices.

3. **Lingering Pain Points**

Despite the 2025 reforms, certain grievances remain consistent:

- **Restaurant & Service Pricing:** Many citizens feel that while GST rates were reduced, many businesses (especially restaurants) increased their "base price," meaning the benefit was not fully passed on to the consumer.
- **Complexity for Small Business Owners:** While the 2025 reforms simplified rates, the "ground-level" compliance dealing with technical glitches on the portal and the requirement for matching invoices

(Input Tax Credit) remains a headache for small shopkeepers.

- **The "Sin Tax" Burden:** Luxury items and "sin goods" (tobacco, aerated drinks) remain at 40% or higher. While generally accepted, the high tax on small "treats" like sodas or mid-range cars is still a point of grumbling for the urban middle class.

Moments of Pride

1. **Nation-Building Through Revenue Mobilisation**

Perhaps the greatest source of pride for the IRS is its silent but decisive contribution to nation-building. Roads, railways, defence preparedness, welfare schemes, disaster relief, and digital infrastructure are sustained by taxes collected with diligence. Every successful assessment, every widened tax base, and every plugged leakage strengthens the fiscal sovereignty of India.

The transformation from a narrow, elite taxpayer base to a more inclusive one especially after economic liberalisation and GST stands as a collective achievement of generations of officers.

2. **Professional Integrity Under Pressure**

Many IRS officers have upheld the law despite immense political, corporate, and social pressure. Instances where officers have resisted illegal instructions, conducted fair assessments against powerful entities, or refused inducements even at personal cost reflect the service's ethical spine.

Transfers, stalled careers, and isolation have often been the price of integrity, but such acts quietly reinforce constitutional governance.

3. **Technological Modernisation**

The shift from manual, discretionary systems to

faceless assessment, e-filing, data analytics, and risk-based scrutiny marks a historic institutional leap. This transition has reduced corruption opportunities, enhanced transparency, and improved taxpayer convenience.

IRS officers played a critical role not merely as implementers but as architects of this digital transformation balancing technology with tax jurisprudence.

4. Crisis Response and Adaptability

During national crises whether economic downturns, pandemics, or natural disasters the IRS has shown flexibility by extending deadlines, rationalising procedures, and prioritising relief over rigid enforcement. This human face of taxation strengthens democratic legitimacy.

5. Intellectual and Judicial Contributions

IRS officers have shaped tax law through reasoned orders, policy inputs, and representation before tribunals and courts. Many landmark judgments rest on careful groundwork laid by field officers who combined legal clarity with factual rigour.

Moments of Regret

1. Excesses of Power

Searches, raids, and coercive recoveries though legally sanctioned have sometimes crossed the line into intimidation. Instances of overreach, selective targeting, or pursuit of revenue targets at the cost of fairness have eroded trust.

Even isolated excesses gain disproportionate public visibility and stain the institution's image.

2. Revenue Over Justice Mindset

At times, the pressure to meet collection targets has led to aggressive assessments, mechanical disallowances, and prolonged litigation often resulting in reversals by appellate authorities. This adversarial approach has burdened honest taxpayers and clogged the judicial system.

Regret lies not in losing cases, but in failing to distinguish evasion from error.

3. Corruption and Ethical Lapses

While the majority serve with integrity, cases of bribery, collusion, and misuse of discretion however few cause disproportionate damage. Corruption within a revenue service strikes at the moral core of governance because it turns law into a commodity.

Each such episode undermines the credibility built by thousands of honest officers.

4. Distance from the Taxpayer

Historically, the IRS has often been seen as remote, intimidating, and opaque. The lack of effective grievance redressal and empathy has sometimes converted compliance into fear rather than civic responsibility.

Regret arises from missed opportunities to build trust as a partner in development rather than merely an enforcer.

5. Internal Pressures and Human Cost

The service has also paid an internal price: stress, burnout, disrupted family lives, and a culture where vulnerability is rarely acknowledged. High-stakes authority combined with public scrutiny has taken a toll on mental and emotional well-being.

An institution that enforces balance must also practice it internally.

Lessons and the Way Forward

Pride and regret are not opposites; they are complementary forces that shape institutional maturity. The future of the IRS lies in:

- Strengthening ethical leadership, not just rule compliance
- Replacing revenue obsession with voluntary compliance philosophy
- Using technology to reduce discretion, not responsibility
- Humanising tax administration without weakening enforcement

The ultimate pride of the IRS will not be measured merely by collections, but by the trust it commands from citizens trust that taxes are assessed fairly, collected honestly, and used wisely.

The journey of the Indian Revenue Service mirrors India's constitutional evolution from colonial authority to democratic accountability. While organisational structures have changed, institutional culture evolves more slowly. The future of the IRS will depend not merely on efficiency or technology, but on legitimacy grounded in fairness, transparency, and constitutional morality.

Anonymous but Common Reality

Many honest IRS officers: Work quietly, never become famous and retire with clean records and respect.Most integrity stories never reach headlines. A Hard Truth. India does not reward honesty loudly, but: It protects consistent honesty over time Institutions remember credibility History judges fairly even if contemporaries don't.

Honest officers often say:

"Once you compromise, the system owns you." Consistency prevents blackmail.

***

The First Posting Where Theory Ends

The first posting in the Indian Revenue Service does not arrive with ceremony. There is no applause, no public oath, no final lesson that neatly bridges theory and reality. It comes instead as an order quietly circulated, a name typed against a designation, a date that looks ordinary until it isn't.

One day you are a probationer arguing case law, underlining statutes, believing that clarity lies somewhere between sections and sub-sections. Next, you are sitting alone behind a desk that has absorbed decades of hesitation, authority, and fear.

Every officer remembers that first desk.

It is rarely new. The wood is scarred. The drawer resists being opened fully. Papers smell faintly of age and damp. Somewhere in those scratches and stains lie decisions that ruined some lives, corrected others, and disappeared without trace. This is where the State ceases to be abstract. This is where it acquires a voice of yours.

The academy had prepared us well, at least in form. We knew the law. We could quote judgments. We understood principles of natural justice and administrative discretion. We were often told, solemnly, that taxation was the price of civilization.

All of it was true. None of it was enough.

The Shock of Ambiguity

The first lesson of the field is ambiguity.

Files arrive incomplete.

Facts are disputed. Explanations are rehearsed. A balance sheet tells different stories depending on who is reading it. The law, once precise, reveals its grey margins. You begin to understand that taxation is not merely an exercise in arithmetic or legality; it is an interpretation of human behaviour conducted under statutory authority.

In training, every problem had a correct answer. In the field, every answer creates another problem.

The corridors of a tax office carry a peculiar stillness. People wait more than they speak. When they do speak, they measure their words. Unlike departments where citizens seek benefits, here they seek relief from scrutiny, from penalty, from uncertainty. Anxiety is the common language.

And the officer, young, cautious, observant becomes its focal point.

The First Case

Every officer remembers the first case that matters.

Mine involved no spectacular sum. It would not attract attention from headquarters. Yet for the taxpayer, it was everything. A small business, inherited rather than built, caught between informal habits and formal law. The books were untidy. The explanations are sincere but incomplete.

The law permitted a strict view. Additions could be made. Penalties initiated. The file could be closed quickly and defensibly.

A senior officer offered advice that was neither cruel nor uncommon: "Be firm in the beginning. People test you."

It was sensible advice. The system respects firmness. Targets exist. Performance is measured. Discretion, though legally recognised, is administratively inconvenient.

Yet something resisted closure. The punishment felt heavier than the fault. The consequences are disproportionate to the intent. That evening, long after office hours, I read the file again not as an officer measured by targets, but as a judge might read it: slowly, skeptically, aware that power had to justify itself.

The final order was balanced. Relief was granted where deserved. Adverse conclusions were recorded where unavoidable. Every decision was reasoned, not assumed.

That file taught me something no lecture ever had: the real test of the IRS is not how much revenue you raise, but how carefully you decide when not to.

Power Without Gratitude

Power in the IRS is vast, legal, and deeply unloved. Few officers possess such authority over private life, the power to summon, to demand explanations years after transactions have occurred, to impose penalties, to initiate searches, even arrests. And yet, this power attracts no admiration. There are no thank-you notes for recoveries, no praise for compliance achieved. At best, there is silence. At worst, hostility. This imbalance shapes the service.

The taxpayer sees coercion where the officer sees enforcement. The media sees harassment where the officer sees statutory duty. The politician sees inconvenience where the officer sees obligation.

Navigating this gulf between intention and perception becomes a quiet, constant strain.

Pressure, Rarely Explicit

Pressure in the IRS seldom arrives as a written order. It comes obliquely. A phone call that offers no instruction but conveys expectation. A file that stops moving. A senior who asks, lightly, whether a matter is "worth pursuing." A name mentioned casually, without context, without command. The young officer must learn to read these silences without surrendering to them.

Too much resistance isolates.

Too much accommodation corrodes. Many falter here not dramatically, but gradually. Compromises are justified as pragmatism. Exceptions become habits. Integrity erodes without collapse.

Others go the opposite way, mistaking harshness for honesty, rigidity for virtue. They alienate colleagues and taxpayers alike, believing that cruelty is courage.

The rare officer learns a harder discipline: firmness anchored in reason, courage anchored in documentation.

The Tyranny of Targets

Revenue targets are unavoidable. Without them, systems decay. But when targets dominate judgment, they deform it.

Not all additions are equal. Some withstand scrutiny; others collapse on appeal. Yet the system often rewards quantity over quality, immediacy over sustainability.

In the first posting, the officer faces an early moral crossroad: chase numbers or chase correctness. Write aggressive orders or defensible ones. Perform today or endure tomorrow.

The academy taught judicial discipline. The field demanded performance metrics. Reconciling the two is perhaps the defining struggle of the service.

Faces Behind Files

The first posting strips abstraction from the word "assessee."

An elderly pensioner was confused by an automated notice. A small trader drowning in compliance. A young professional frightened by a technical default. A corporate representative who speaks in power rather than law. One afternoon, a retired schoolteacher walked in unannounced, clutching a thin file tied with string. He had received a notice he did not understand. His income barely crossed the threshold. He had no representative.

The issue was trivial. The solution is simple. But the encounter lingered. It was a reminder that the tax system, for all its sophistication, is experienced by citizens as something personal and often frightening.

Moments like these rarely find place in official records. But they shape the inner compass of those who notice them.

Lessons the Law Cannot Teach

The law does not teach you how to refuse politely. It does not teach you how to endure insinuation. It does not teach you how to live with fear of vigilance, of transfers, of retrospective judgment. These lessons come informally, often from seniors who choose to mentor rather than instruct.

"Write every order as if you will have to defend it alone," one advised.

It was the most honest guidance I received.

The Sound of Silence

Power rarely announces itself in the Indian Revenue Service.When it does, it is unmistakable and usually dangerous.

Most of the time, it arrives in silence.

Not the benign silence of routine, but the deliberate quiet that follows a file which should have moved and did not. A proposal that received neither approval nor rejection. A question that was never answered. In the IRS, silence is not absence. It is instruction stripped of responsibility. By the time an officer reaches this stage, he has learned to listen for it.

When Orders Are Not Written

The training academy teaches hierarchy. The

field teaches nuance. Written orders are safe. They can be followed, questioned, or challenged. What unsettles officers are situations where instructions are implied rather than issued where a senior says nothing, but expects compliance; where a conversation ends just before clarity arrives.

"Use your judgment," a superior may say, carefully.

Judgment, in such moments, is not about law. It is about alignment.

The young officer learns that the most consequential decisions are often made without words. The system functions not only through files and notings, but through shared understanding of what must not be pursued too vigorously, what must be delayed, and what must be closed quietly.

These understandings are never recorded. They are absorbed.

The First 'Sensitive' Case

Every IRS officer encounters, sooner or later, what is informally called a sensitive case.

It is not always large in monetary terms. Its sensitivity lies elsewhere in the name attached to it, the timing, the political climate, or the institutional discomfort it creates.

The file looks ordinary at first. The law applies as it always has. The facts raise legitimate questions. And yet, the atmosphere around it feels different. Calls are returned more slowly. Meetings are postponed. Guidance becomes evasive. No one tells you to stop. No one tells you to proceed. You are left to interpret the silence.

This is the moment when neutrality becomes difficult and courage complicated. To proceed is legally defensible. To pause is administratively convenient. Both choices carry risk. The officer learns that the most dangerous position in the IRS is not being wrong, but being alone.

Alignment and the Illusion of Choice

Alignment is a word often used without definition.

It does not necessarily mean acting illegally. More often, it means choosing which lawful options to exercise and which to ignore. The law provides a spectrum of responses from aggressive to restrained. Alignment is about selecting the response that best fits the unspoken expectation of the moment.

This is where the system tests character most subtly.

An officer who consistently chooses restraint may be seen as sensible or pliable. One who consistently chooses aggression may be seen as upright or reckless. Labels are fluid; reputations are fragile.

What complicates matters further is that expectations shift. What is encouraged today may be questioned tomorrow. Political climates change faster than files close.

The officer begins to understand that institutional memory is selective, and loyalty is temporal.

The Cost of Visibility

Visibility is dangerous in this phase.

Officers who become associated with controversial cases whether rightly or wrongly find their careers acquiring an edge. Transfers arrive unexpectedly. Opportunities dry up quietly. Deputations are deferred without explanation.

Nothing punitive enough to challenge. Nothing explicit enough to prove. The message is clear without being spoken. Some officers respond by withdrawing or avoiding complex files, seeking low-profile postings, reducing decision-making to the minimum required. Others double down, convinced that legality will protect them.

The system tolerates both, but rewards neither consistently.

Silence as a Shield

Silence is not always coercive. Sometimes, it is protective. A senior officer may choose not to intervene in a difficult case, allowing a junior to act independently. This silence grants autonomy without endorsement. If the decision succeeds, it stands on merit. If it fails, it stands alone. Such silences are calculated. They preserve deniability while permitting action.

Understanding this distinction between hostile silence and enabling silence is part of institutional literacy. It cannot be taught. It is learned through bruises.

Ethics Without Applause

Ethical decisions in the IRS rarely attract recognition. Proceeding against a powerful entity lawfully may earn private admiration but public inconvenience. Restraining oneself where aggression is popular may invite criticism. Doing the right thing often pleases no one immediately. The officer learns that ethics in this service is not about heroism. It is about continuity, acting in ways one can defend years later, in writing, without anger or apology.

This is a lonely ethic. It offers no guarantees.

The Slow Education of Courage

Courage changes shape

It is no longer the courage to decide, but the courage to persist. To keep files alive when they are meant to fade. To ask questions that receive no answers. To record dissent without dramatizing it.

Some officers discover a quiet defiance here not loud enough to provoke, not soft enough to disappear. Others retreat into safety, convincing themselves that discretion is wisdom.

The service accommodates both. History judges neither kindly nor harshly. It mostly forgets.

When Silence Finally Speaks

Occasionally, silence breaks.

A call arrives late in the evening. A meeting is suddenly scheduled. A file moves after months of stillness. The officer realises that the system has decided without announcing how or why.

At such moments, resistance is futile and compliance feels empty. The officer executes what is required, carefully, legally, without enthusiasm.

This is not corruption. It is an accommodation.

Understanding this difference is essential to surviving the service without illusions.

The Boundary Revealed

Now, the officer has learned where the real boundaries lie, not the written ones, but the operational ones.

He understands that power in the IRS is negotiated daily, quietly, invisibly. That silence can command more effectively than instruction. That courage must sometimes be slow, sometimes silent, sometimes strategic.

He also understands something else, more unsettling: that the system rarely asks for wrongdoing. It asks for restraint at convenient moments.

Whether that restraint is wisdom or weakness is a question each officer answers privately.

The End of Innocence

By the end of the first posting, the probationer disappears.

In his place stands an officer still uncertain, still learning, but no longer naïve. He understands that the IRS is not a monolith but a fragile accumulation of daily decisions. That integrity is not an announcement, but a habit formed quietly. That every file is a test not merely of law, but of character.

Years later, designations will change. Offices will grow larger. Files will become heavier.

But somewhere, in an unremarkable building, a desk still remembers his first signature.

And he remembers the moment he learned that theory does not end where practice begins but where conscience intervenes.

That is the real first posting of the Indian Revenue Service.

***

Raids, Searches, and the heatre of Authority

Taxes are hated by almost everyone not because people deny the need for public money, but because taxes are where the citizen most directly feels the power of the state. Taxes are hated not because they exist, but because they sit at the uncomfortable intersection of money, power, fairness, and trust where no government can ever fully please everyone. No one wakes up excited to pay taxes. They are seen as an involuntary transfer of hard-earned income, imposed by law, enforced by penalties, and often paid long before any visible benefit is felt. Unlike prices, which are linked to choice, taxes are compulsory. That single fact makes them emotionally unpopular across income groups, professions, and political beliefs. For the ordinary citizen, taxes reduce disposable income and complicate everyday decisions, what to buy, how to save, whether to invest. For small businesses and professionals, taxes mean compliance costs, paperwork, audits, and the constant fear of interpretational disputes. For the wealthy, taxes are viewed as punishment for success. Each group dislikes taxes for different reasons, but the resentment is universal.

The dislike is amplified when taxpayers feel that the burden is unfairly distributed or poorly explained. Indirect taxes like GST are hated because they are paid silently with every purchase, hurting the poor and middle class the most. Direct taxes are disliked because they are visible, deducted upfront, and often accompanied by complex rules and changing exemptions. When public services appear inadequate, bad roads, overcrowded hospitals, weak policing, the question "what am I getting in return?" becomes sharper. Taxes are also unpopular because the benefits are collective and long-term, while the cost is individual and immediate. A taxpayer pays today, but the returns for better infrastructure, social security, national defence are diffuse and often invisible. Success is taken for granted; failure is immediately blamed on the tax system.

Yet, paradoxically, societies demand more from governments while hating the taxes required to fund those demands. This tension is permanent and unavoidable. The challenge for any tax system is not to make taxes lovable that is impossible but to make them appear fair, simple, transparent, and visibly linked to public outcomes. When trust in the state is high, taxes are tolerated. When trust is low, even low taxes feel oppressive.

It is a universal truth that nobody enjoys seeing their hard-earned money disappear before it hits their bank account. However, "hating" taxes is a complex emotional and economic response that goes beyond just wanting to keep more cash. Psychologically, taxes feel like a loss rather than a purchase. When you buy a coffee, you get a tangible product immediately. When you pay taxes, the "product" (road maintenance, national defense, public schools) is often invisible or taken for granted. This creates a sense of losing wealth without an immediate, equivalent reward. For many, it isn't just the amount of money, it's the effort required to pay it. Navigating tax codes can feel like learning a second language. The fear of making an honest mistake and facing an audit or penalty adds a layer of stress to the financial cost. A major driver of "tax hate" is the belief that the money is being mismanaged. Citizens have no direct say in exactly how their specific dollars are spent. Seeing "bridge to nowhere" projects or inefficient government programs leads to the feeling that tax dollars are being dropped into a black hole. Taxes represent a fundamental tension between Individualism and Collectivism:-

Individualism: "I earned this; it belongs to me and my family."

Collectivism: "We live in a society; we must pool resources to function."

Even those who support social safety nets often feel a biological "itch" of resentment when their personal resources are diverted to the group. Despite the universal grumbling, most people also "hate" the alternative: crumbling infrastructure, no emergency services, and a lack of public order. As Oliver Wendell Holmes Jr. famously put it:

"Taxes are what we pay for civilized society."

We might hate the bill, but we generally enjoy the amenities that come with the subscription.

If you thought modern tax was a headache, history's tax collectors were far more "creative." In the past, governments didn't just tax what you earned; they taxed how you lived, what you wore, and even how you looked.

Here are some of the most bizarre historical taxes that turned daily life into a strategic game of avoidance.

1. **The Window Tax (England & Scotland, 1696)**

This is perhaps the most famous "stupid" tax. The government wanted to tax the wealthy without the controversy of an income tax. Since big houses had more windows, windows became the proxy for wealth. As a consequence people didn't want to pay, so they brick up their windows. You can still see "blind windows" (bricked-up window frames) on old buildings in London and Edinburgh today. It eventually led to health issues due to a lack of light and ventilation, earning it the nickname "a tax on light and air."

2. **The Beard Tax (Russia, 1698)**

Emperor Peter the Great wanted to modernize Russia and make it look more like Western Europe. To him, traditional Russian beards looked "old-fashioned." If you wanted to keep your beard, you had to pay a hefty annual tax.

Once you paid, you were given a copper or silver "beard token" that you had to carry at all times to prove your facial hair was legal. It featured an image of a beard and the phrase "The beard is a useless burden."

3. **The Brick Tax (Great Britain, 1784)**

To help pay for the American Revolutionary War, the British government decided to tax bricks.The builders realized that if they used larger bricks, they would need fewer of them and therefore pay less taxes, then the government caught on and eventually capped the legal size of a brick. This is why many buildings from this era have noticeably oversized bricks.

4. **The Salt Tax (France - The Gabelle**

This wasn't just a tax; it was a forced purchase. Salt was essential for preserving food, so the French government made it a state monopoly. Every citizen over the age of seven was required to buy a certain amount of salt every week at a price fixed by the king. As a result, it was so deeply hated and seen as so unfair that it became one of the primary catalysts for the French Revolution.

People don't hate paying taxes; they hate feeling cheated, harassed, or ignored. If you fix those emotions, compliance rises almost automatically. Getting citizens to pay taxes honestly isn't just about the "stick" (penalties); it's often about the "carrot" (services) and the "mirror" (social norms). Behavioral science and economics suggest that a multi-pronged approach balancing trust, simplicity, and deterrence is the most effective way to foster a culture of voluntary compliance.

Here's a practical, citizen-centric way to encourage people to pay the right amount of tax (not more, not less):-

1. **Make Taxes Feel Fair, Not Arbitrary**

Fairness is the single biggest driver of compliance. Build "Tax Morale" through Transparency

- Citizens are more likely to pay when they feel their money isn't disappearing into a black hole.
- Show the "Return on Investment": Governments that provide clear, visual breakdowns of how tax dollars are spent (e.g., "Your $1,000 paid for 5 meters of this new highway") see higher compliance.
- Publicize Benefits: Highlighting tangible public goods like new schools, parks, or emergency services, links the act of paying to a positive outcome. Combat corruption and trust is the bedrock of taxation. When citizens see officials being held accountable for the misuse of funds, their own willingness to pay honestly increases. Visible action against big evaders (not just small taxpayers) builds moral pressure
- Reduce frequent rate changes and exemptions that benefit a few

Ensure similar incomes are taxed similarly, regardless of profession. When citizens believe "everyone is paying their share," honesty goes up.

2. **Simplify Ruthlessly**

Complexity is the enemy of compliance.

- Pre-filled returns using employer, bank, GST, and TDS data
- One-page summaries:

Income → Deductions → Tax due → Why

- Fewer forms, fewer notices, fewer logins

India's recent ITR simplification and faceless systems are steps in the right direction but they must feel human, not robotic.

3. **Shift from "Fear" to "Trust"**

Fear gets short-term results; trust gets voluntary compliance.

- Treat first-time errors as mistakes, not crimes
- Use nudges:

  "9 out of 10 people in your income group filed on time"
- Clear, polite language in notices (no legalese intimidation)

Behavioral economics works, people follow norms more than threats.

4. **Show Citizens What Their Taxes Do**

People pay more willingly when they see outcomes.

Annual "Taxpayer Report Card":

- ₹100 paid → roads, schools, defence, healthcare

Hyper-local impact dashboards:

- "Your ward's streetlights / hospital upgrades funded by taxes"

Taxes stop feeling like loss and start feeling like contribution.

5. **Reward Honesty-**

Compliance should have visible benefits.

- Faster refunds for clean filers
- Lower scrutiny frequency for consistently honest taxpayers
- Priority services (passports, licenses, MSME credit) linked to tax history

Make honesty the easier and smarter choice.

6. **Reduce Cash, Increase Digital Trails**

Don't preach but design the system.

- Incentivise digital payments for small merchants
- Link high-value consumption (travel, property, luxury) with tax reporting
- Use analytics to flag risk, not to randomly harass

The goal is certainty of detection, not fear of raids. Respect the Taxpayer's Dignity. This is underrated and powerful. Time-bound grievance redressal.

Accountability for tax officials' misconduct

Clear appeal mechanisms without endless litigation. People comply more when the state behaves like a partner, not a predator. Tax Literacy as Civic Education, Long-term but transformative.

Simple school modules:

- "Why taxes exist"
- "What happens if everyone evades"

Real-life examples instead of theory

You don't raise honest taxpayers overnight, you raise them.

Small changes in communication can have a massive impact on behavior.

- **The Social Norm Effect:** Including a simple sentence in tax reminders like "9 out of 10 people in your community pay their taxes on time" creates a psychological urge to conform to the "honest" majority.
- **Moral Reminders:** Proactive messages that emphasize the "civic duty" or the moral importance of honesty before the filing deadline have been shown to reduce under-reporting.
- **Personalization:** Sending personalized letters or emails rather than generic forms makes the obligation feel more direct and less like an automated system.

Complexity is a major barrier to honesty. If the process is a nightmare, people are more tempted to cut corners.

- **Simplify the Code:** Use "plain language" instead of legal jargon. In some countries, the government pre-fills tax returns with known data (like salary), leaving the citizen to simply verify. This reduces errors and the "temptation" to hide known income. User-friendly mobile apps and online portals with 24/7 support reduces the "compliance cost" (the time and effort required to pay). If people feel the system is "rigged" for the wealthy or well-connected, they will justify their own dishonesty. Auditing high-net-worth individuals and large corporations publicly (within legal limits) proves that the rules apply to everyone. Ensuring that two people in the same financial situation are taxed exactly the same way prevents feelings of resentment. While trust is key, a credible threat of being caught is still necessary for those who view tax as a simple "cost-benefit" calculation.
- **Smart Audits:** Using data analytics to flag inconsistencies makes the "probability of detection" feel higher. Letting taxpayers know that the government is receiving data from third parties (like banks or employers) gently signals that hiding income is difficult.

The Core Insight is People pay taxes not because they must, but because they believe the system is worth cooperating with.

Enforcement matters but legitimacy matters more. From inside the tax system, one truth is obvious but rarely said aloud: most citizens are not habitual evaders. They are cautious, confused, or mistrustful. The system loses more revenue to fear, complexity, and poor communication than to outright fraud. It is well known that:

A small minority of chronic evaders account for a disproportionate share of revenue loss

Large, well-advised entities exploit ambiguity and litigation delays. Meanwhile, small and honest taxpayers often overpay or disengage out of anxiety. Yet enforcement energy historically flows downward because small taxpayers are easier, quicker, and safer to pursue. This creates a silent paradox:

The more compliant you are, the more visible and vulnerable you become.

Administratively, notices are often issued:

- based on data mismatches, not proof of evasion, through automated systems with minimal human context, using language drafted for legal defensibility, not citizen comprehension. Officers know many notices will be resolved with no additional tax payable, yet the psychological cost to the taxpayer is enormous, missed workdays, professional fees, and stress. A system that scares honest taxpayers unintentionally trains them to:
- Underreport to stay "below the radar," or Exit the formal system altogether.

Tax administrators operate under:

- Revenue targets, often annual and non-negotiable
- Audit metrics that reward quantity of action, not quality
- Personal accountability risks if a case is dropped but little reward for restraint

This creates a bias toward defensive enforcement:

"It is safer to issue a notice than to explain later why one wasn't."

Reform must therefore protect good administrative judgment, not just taxpayers. From inside the system, the following approaches work far better than raids and penalties:

- Early, non-adversarial communication
- A simple clarification letter resolves more cases than formal scrutiny
- Predictable treatment
- When similar cases are handled similarly, word spreads fast
- Respectful interaction
- A taxpayer who feels heard rarely becomes non-compliant later

Officers often observe that once trust is broken, even honest taxpayers become defensive forever.

Nothing builds credibility like:

- Timely refunds
- Clear explanations of adjustments
- Apologies for departmental errors

Inside tax departments, delayed refunds are recognized as one of the biggest self-inflicted credibility losses yet they persist due to procedural caution and fear of audit objections.

The Quiet Truth About Voluntary Compliance

Voluntary compliance rises not when penalties increase, but when:

- Detection is certain but reasonable
- Enforcement is selective but fair
- The honest majority feels protected, not suspected.

Tax officers know this instinctively. What they need is a system that aligns administrative incentives with citizen trust.

A tax system does not fail because citizens are dishonest. It fails when honesty feels unsafe. Encouraging citizens to pay the right tax is less about stronger laws and more about calmer administration, clearer communication, and institutional empathy.

Interestingly, GST enforcement investigations are showing comparatively higher detection, recovery, and prosecution success than traditional corruption cases under vigilance or anti-corruption laws.

The reason lies in structural design differences, not merely officer efficiency.

1. **Evidence is System-Generated, Not Human-Dependent**

   Traditional corruption cases depend on:

- complainants,
- trap witnesses,
- oral testimony.

These frequently fail in court.

In contrast, GST investigations rely on digital audit trails generated automatically through the Goods and Services Tax Network (GSTN):

- Invoices,
- E-way bills,
- Return filings,
- Input tax credit chains,
- Banking linkage.

Evidence exists before investigation begins.

Result: Less dependence on hostile witnesses.

2. **Data Analytics Instead of Complaint-Based Policing**

Anti-corruption agencies act reactively after complaints.

GST enforcement works proactively using:

- Risk profiling,
- AI-based mismatch detection,
- Network analysis of fake firms.

Systems like invoice matching automatically expose fraud patterns such as:

- Fake ITC,
- Circular trading,
- Shell entities.

Digital anomalies are harder to deny in court.

3. Financial Trail is Central to GST Law

Under the Central Goods and Services Tax Act, 2017, offences are fundamentally economic and document-driven.

Key advantage: Tax liability itself becomes primary evidence.

Unlike corruption cases where intent must be proved, GST cases often hinge on:

- Wrongful availment,
- Tax evasion,
- Fraudulent documentation.

Objective records replace subjective intent arguments.

4. Reduced Need to Prove "Mens Rea"

Under the Prevention of Corruption Act, 1988:

- Demand,
- Acceptance,
- Motive

Must be proven.

In GST offences:

- Fake invoice issuance,
- Non-existent supply,
- Wrongful ITC claim

Create statutory presumptions once documentary fraud is established.

This significantly improves prosecution sustainability.

5. **Immediate Financial Consequences**

GST enforcement allows:

- Attachment of bank accounts,
- Blocking of ITC,
- Provisional attachment of property.

Recovery often happens before trial completion.

Traditional corruption cases:

- Wait years for conviction before recovery.

Economic pressure induces voluntary compliance or settlement.

6. **Technology Minimises Discretion**

Classic corruption enforcement involves high field discretion.

GST architecture:

- Standardised filings,
- Automated alerts,
- digital verification, reduces subjective decision-making.

Less discretion → fewer procedural challenges in court.

7. **Parallel Civil + Criminal Proceedings**

GST law enables simultaneous:

- Tax demand,
- Penalty,
- Prosecution.

Even if criminal conviction is delayed, civil recovery succeeds.

Anti-corruption prosecution usually has only criminal consequence, raising evidentiary burden.

8. Documentary Chain of Conspiracy

Fake GST fraud typically involves networks:

- Suppliers,
- Transporters,
- Beneficiaries,
- Banking channels.

Digital linkage creates conspiracy mapping, strengthening prosecution narratives.

In corruption cases, conspiracy is often inferred, not digitally demonstrated.

9. Institutional Learning & Specialisation

Post-GST, officers trained through National Academy of Customs, Indirect Taxes and Narcotics (NACIN) increasingly use:

- forensic accounting,
- data mining,
- financial intelligence analysis.

Traditional vigilance investigation still relies heavily on policing models developed decades ago.

10. Key Lessons for Anti-Corruption Agencies

Anti-corruption bodies can adapt GST-style enforcement principles:

Shift from Trap-Based to Data-Based Investigation

- Use transaction analytics instead of complaint traps.

Build Digital Asset & Lifestyle Analytics

- Compare income, assets, procurement decisions digitally.

Follow Money, Not Statements

- Financial intelligence should precede interrogation.

Integrate Databases

- Link taxation, property, banking, and procurement data.

Early Financial Freezing

- Economic consequences improve enforcement credibility.

Specialised Economic Prosecutors

- Trial strategy must begin during the investigation itself.

Strategic Insight

GST represents a shift from "person-centric investigation" to "system-centric enforcement."

Future anti-corruption success in India will likely depend on:

- Algorithmic detection + financial forensics + procedural integrity.

Low conviction rates in corruption cases in India are not due to one agency or one weakness. They arise from structural, legal, institutional, and behavioural problems across the entire criminal-justice chain.

For enforcement agencies like CBI and vigilance bodies, this is a critical governance concern.

Extremely high legal Standard of Proof

Under criminal law, corruption must be proved "beyond reasonable doubt."

Cases registered under the Prevention of Corruption Act, 1988 require proof of:

Demand of bribe, acceptance, recovery and intent (quid-pro-quo). If even one element fails, courts give benefit. Courts repeatedly hold that mere recovery of money is insufficient without proof of demand. Many technically weak cases collapse during trial.

Poor evidence collection & investigation design. Corruption today is rarely cash-in-hand bribery. Modern corruption involves: layered transactions, shell companies, benami ownership, digital transfers, and policy manipulation rather than direct payment.

A raid is never just a raid.

On paper, it is a statutory instrument precise, conditional, hedged with safeguards. In practice, it is theatre: visible, symbolic, and unforgettable. For the taxpayer, it is shock. For the media, spectacle. For the system, assertion.

For the officer, it is something else entirely a convergence of law, fear, responsibility, and irreversible consequence.

No one forgets their first search.

Raids begin long before doors are knocked.

They start as fragments an intelligence input, an unusual transaction, a pattern that does not quite align. Information arrives indirectly, rarely complete, often unverified. It must be assessed, corroborated, weighed.

The law demands "reason to believe," not suspicion, not pressure, not curiosity. That phrase reason to believe is both shield and sword. It protects citizens from arbitrary intrusion, and officers from accusation. But it is also fragile.

Poorly recorded, it collapses. Poorly conceived, it becomes indefensible.

In the weeks before a search, the officer lives in a state of heightened watchfulness. Conversations are guarded. Files are handled discreetly. Not because secrecy is glamorous, but because leaks are fatal. A compromised raid is worse than no raid at all.

This phase is invisible to the public. Yet it is where most errors occur.

Authority in Motion

The morning of a raid carries its own silence.

Teams assemble early, before offices open and phones ring freely. Faces are serious, not dramatic. There is no triumph in the air, only concentration. Each officer knows that once the door opens, control begins to leak.

The law prescribes conduct meticulously presence of witnesses, scope of search, respect for dignity. In training, this seems straightforward. In reality, emotions distort procedure.

There are moments when a subject pleads, moments when they threaten, moments when they pretend indifference. There are family members watching silently, staff unsure whether to cooperate or obstruct. There is the weight of being watched by those present, by colleagues, by the institution itself.

Authority, at this moment, is fragile. Too soft, and the search loses meaning. Too harsh, and it becomes abuse.

The officer must perform restraint as convincingly as power. Raids attract audiences, even when none are invited. Neighbours gather discreetly. Phones appear. Stories travel faster than facts. By the time the search concludes, narratives have already formed. To the public, a raid implies guilt. To the law, it proves nothing. This distinction is rarely appreciated.

The media, hungry for immediacy, reduces complexity to visuals boxes carried out, sealed rooms, officials standing guard. The taxpayer becomes a character, not a citizen. The officer becomes an enforcer, not an adjudicator. Inside the service, this spectacle is uncomfortable. Raids are not victories. They are the beginnings of scrutiny, litigation, explanation. Yet once visibility enters, restraint becomes harder. Expectations grow. Silence is interpreted as weakness. The theatre demands an ending. The law demands patience.

The Myth of Discovery

Popular imagination treats raids as treasure hunts. In reality, most searches produce documents, not drama. Ledgers, digital devices, transaction records evidence that requires months of analysis. Cash seizures, when they occur, are often incidental, not central. What matters is not what is found, but what can be proven, sustained, defended.

This is where many cases falter. Evidence gathered dramatically may prove legally fragile. Statements recorded under pressure unravel. Digital data, improperly handled, becomes inadmissible.The officer learns, often painfully, that force creates visibility, but documentation creates sustainability.

After the Applause

Once the search concludes, the real work begins. The team disperses. The subject retreats into legal counsel. The media moves on. Only the files remain voluminous, complex, unforgiving. Every action during the raid will now be examined: Were safeguards followed? Was scope exceeded? Were rights respected? Was dignity preserved? Any lapse, however minor, becomes leverage. The officer learns that raids are judged not by their intent, but by their weakest procedural moment. This is where reputations are made or quietly damaged.

The Officer as Symbol

Raids transform officers into symbols.

To some, they are agents of justice. To others, instruments of intimidation. Rarely are they seen as administrators bound by law.

This symbolic weight is unfair, but unavoidable. The officer must carry it without defensiveness.

Inside, however, the toll is real. There is no applause when procedures are followed flawlessly. There is only silence until something goes wrong.

The Ethics of Intrusion

Searches force officers to confront the most uncomfortable truth of their power: the law permits intrusion into private life.

Bedrooms are opened. Personal devices examined. Family routines disrupted.

Even when legally justified, this intrusion demands ethical restraint. The officer must remember that enforcement is not humiliation. That authority does not extend to cruelty. That dignity is not a concession.

Those who forget this lose something irretrievable, long before vigilance notices.

When Raids Are Questioned

Not all raids survive scrutiny.

Some collapse under judicial review. Others falter due to procedural lapses. When this happens, the officer faces not only legal consequences, but existential doubt.

Was the information faulty? Was the pressure too great? Was ambition mistaken for duty?

These questions have no institutional forum. They are answered privately, if at all.

The service moves on. The officer carries the memory.

The Quiet Aftermath

Long after headlines fade, the officer remains bound to the raid.

Notings must be written. Evidence analysed. Assessments framed. Appeals defended. Years may pass before closure arrives, if it ever does.

This prolonged accountability tempers enthusiasm. It teaches caution. It reminds the officer that a raid is not an event, but a commitment one that consumes time, credibility, and emotional energy.

Raids reveal much about taxpayers, systems, and officers. They reveal how institutions respond under pressure. How quickly narratives outrun facts. How power attracts distortion.Most of all, they reveal the officer to himself. Some emerge more careful, more disciplined, less impressed by spectacle. Others emerge cynical, convinced that visibility matters more than correctness.

The difference shapes careers.

The officer understands now that raids are not the pinnacle of authority, but its most exposed edge. That true strength lies not in intrusion, but in restraint exercised invisibly.

The theatre of authority may satisfy public appetite.

The discipline of administration sustains institutions.

GST Status Quo

The CAG in its report State Finances 2023 -24 allows a clear comparison of state revenues before and after GST implementation. Status that are adopting effectively to the GST physical architecture and those that are not. At the aggregate level the picture appears modest. In real terms combined revenue of a state grew by about 2% in 2023- 24. But headline numbers obscure what matters most, divergence. Some status including Bihar, Gujarat MP, and UP recorded revenue growth of 6% or more. Others such as Karnataka, Rajasthan and West Bengal saw real decline. Even in Maharashtra, India's most economically advanced state, posted near stagnant growth. This widening gap is not incidental, it reflects differences in how states are building or failing to build their own revenue capacity. For years, a key concern about GST was that it would centralise fiscal power and weaken State autonomy. But medium term evidence now points to a balanced conclusion. GST has in fact, strengthened Status tax performance. Gains, however have been uneven.

In 2018-19, the first year reflecting the full impact of GST state GST (SGST)accounted for about 41% of a States on tax revenue (SOTR). By 2023 -24 this had risen to 43%. Average annual growth in SOTR increased from around 9.5% in the pre GST period to 11.7% since SGST itself grew at an average annual rate of about 13%. These trends suggest that GST has made state tax revenue more buoyant. Improvements in compliance systems, in voice matching and formalisation of economic activity have expanded effective tax base. In that sense GST has delivered more than many critics anticipated. GST has helped States but it has not compensated for weak fiscal management. New data makes it clear that States can still under perform even when GST collection remain robust. That is because fiscal strength depends on more than SGST. It also hinges on non tax revenue (NTR), asset monetization, returns from PSU and balance between self government generated resources and Government of India's transfers. Karnataka illustrates this complexity. It remains one of the most fiscally self reliant States with their own tax revenue contributing around 70% of the total revenue, well above the national average of roughly 50%. Yet,. it recorded a real decline in total revenue in 2023- 24. A strong tax base was not enough to offset weakening non tax revenues and it reduced asset monetization. The situation is more concerning in Rajasthan and West Bengal. Both States combined relatively weak own tax shares with declining non tax revenues and higher dependency on Central transfer, a fiscally fragile mix. Closure look at a States with declining revenue reveals a common pattern with a fall in the share of NTR. This component which includes dividends from state public enterprises, royalties from natural resources, user charges and income from land and forests reflects a States ability to monetize assets and enforce pricing discipline. Persistence weakness here signals a structural problem rather than a cyclical one.

Composition of tax revenues also offers important insights. West Bengal for instance derives a relatively large share of its own tax revenue about 45%, from SGST. Karnataka and Rajasthan show similar patterns though slightly lesser extent. While higher SGST share can indicate strong domestic economic activity in the West Bengal case. It coexists with a weak tax base. This points to deeper issues in translating economic activity into sustain fiscal strength. In contrast, UP presents a note worthy shift as one of the stronger performers in 2023-24 .Its revenue growth appears to be supported not by GST but also by other taxes and excise. This diversification is critical. States that rely on a broader revenue base are better equipped to manage shocks. The broader lesson is becoming clear. GST has worked better for the States than many expected. Rise in SGST share, acceleration in SOTR growth and sustained expansion of GST collections point to improved tax buoyancy .

Offence under the GST Act

The GST Act in India identifies 21 specific offences under Section 122 of the CGST Act. These range from simple procedural lapses to high-value criminal fraud. As of early 2026, the Indian government has significantly ramped up technology-driven enforcement, detecting over 24,000 cases of fake invoicing in the current fiscal year alone.

1. **Major Categories of Offences**

- **Fake Invoicing:** Issuing an invoice without an actual supply of goods to "pass on" Input Tax Credit (ITC).A firm issues invoices worth crore to multiple buyers without actually supplying goods only to help them claim Input Tax Credit (ITC). Penalties are- 100% of tax evaded or ₹10,000 (whichever is higher).

- **ITC Fraud:** Availing Input Tax Credit using fake invoices or invoices from "non-existent" suppliers. A trader claims ITC based on invoices from a supplier who doesn't exist or is a shell company. Penalties are same as above; also liable for arrest if > ₹2 Crore.

- **Tax Evasion:** Deliberately suppressing sales turnover or under-reporting the value of supplies. A restaurant shows only ₹50 lakh turnover in GST returns but actual turnover is ₹1.5 crore (remaining collected in cash). Penalties are- 100% of tax amount (Fraud case) or 10% (Non-fraud).

- **Non-Registration:** Operating a business without GST registration despite crossing the turnover threshold. A business crosses ₹40 lakh turnover but continues operations without GST registration. Penalty - 100% of tax due or ₹10,000.

- **Inaccurate Records:** Failing to maintain financial records/books or providing false information during an audit. Fixed penalty up to ₹25,000.

- **Obstruction:** Preventing an officer from performing their duties or failing to appear on a summons. During inspection, the taxpayer refuses access to records or hides documents. Penalty up to ₹25,000.

2. Recent Landmark Case Studies (2025-2026)

The "Sleeping Modules" Case (Dec 2025): Authorities uncovered a massive network of "dormant" shell companies. These entities were registered and left inactive for months before being suddenly "activated" to circulate billions in fake ITC before disappearing.

Real Estate Under-valuation (Mumbai/Bengaluru): A major developer was caught collecting GST from homebuyers but not remitting it to the government, claiming it was offset by ITC on construction materials that were later found to be fictitious.

The Supreme Court Ruling on "Consolidated Notices" (Jan 2026): In a recent shift, the Supreme Court allowed tax authorities to issue consolidated show-cause notices for multiple years in cases involving fraud (Section 74), making it harder for serial offenders to escape on technical time-limit grounds.

Most high-value GST frauds today involve ITC fraud networks, such as:

- Fake firms
- Circular trading
- Invoice layering

These are often uncovered through:

- Data analytics (GSTN)
- E-way bill mismatch
- Return discrepancies (GSTR-1 vs GSTR-3B)

3. Criminal Liabilities & Jail Terms

GST offences become cognizable and non-bailable if the tax amount involved is high.

- ₹1 Crore – ₹2 Crore: Up to 1 year imprisonment + Fine.

- ₹2 Crore – ₹5 Crore: Up to 3 years imprisonment + Fine.
- Above ₹5 Crore: Up to 5 years imprisonment + Fine.

Note:

Even if you aren't the primary offender but you "aid or abet" a GST fraud (e.g., an accountant knowingly helping a client create fake bills), you can be personally fined up to ₹25,000.

Here are real-world style GST investigation case studies based on actual enforcement patterns and reported cases in India under the Central Goods and Services Tax Act, 2017. I've simplified them into structured formats useful for exams, training, and practical understanding.

- **Case Study 1:** Fake ITC Racket via Shell Companies

(Pattern widely detected by GST intelligence units)

Facts:

A network of ~120 firms across multiple states (Delhi, Gujarat, Maharashtra) was created using fake PAN/ Aadhaar. These firms issued invoices without actual supply of goods.

Modus Operandi:

Creation of dummy firms using poor individuals' identities

- No physical business activity
- Circular billing to inflate turnover
- Passing fake ITC to real businesses

Amount Involved:

₹800+ crore fake ITC

Detection:

- No e-way bills

- Same IP address used for multiple GST registrations
- No transport records

Outcome:

- Mastermind arrested
- Multiple GST registrations cancelled
- ITC reversed + prosecution under Section 132
- **Case Study 2:** Steel Trader Suppressing Turnover

(Typical enforcement case)

Facts:

A steel trader declared turnover of ₹3 crore, but actual bank deposits indicated ₹12 crore.

Modus Operandi:

- Cash sales not recorded in GST returns
- Parallel books of accounts maintained

Detection:

- Bank statement analysis
- Mismatch between GSTR-3B and actual inflows

Outcome:

- Tax + penalty recovered
- Prosecution initiated
- **Case Study 3:** Fake Export Refund Scam

(Export fraud case pattern)

Facts:

A company claimed IGST refund on exports worth ₹150 crore.

Modus Operandi:

- Inflated invoices for exports
- Goods either low value or never exported

- Use of related foreign entities

Detection:

- Customs-GST data mismatch
- Unrealistic pricing compared to market rates

Outcome:

- Refund blocked
- Firm blacklisted
- Directors arrested
- **Case Study 4:** E-Way Bill Fraud in Transport Sector

Facts:

A logistics company generated e-way bills without actual movement of goods.

Modus Operandi:

- Recycling same vehicle numbers
- Fake transport documentation
- Supporting fake ITC chains

Detection:

- Same truck used simultaneously in multiple states
- GPS mismatch

Outcome:

- ITC chain busted
- Penalty + arrests
- **Case Study 5:** Restaurant Collecting GST but Not Depositing

Facts:

A chain of restaurants collected GST from customers but failed to deposit it for over 1 year.

Modus Operandi:

- Charging GST on bills
- Not filing returns regularly
- Using collected tax as working capital

Detection:

- Customer complaints
- Return filing mismatch

Outcome:

- Recovery of dues
- Prosecution initiated
- **Case Study 6:** Bogus Billing in Textile Sector (Common in Surat/Bhiwandi clusters)

Facts:

Multiple textile traders engaged in circular trading to inflate ITC.

Modus Operandi:

- Same goods rotated across firms
- No actual value addition
- Fake invoices to claim ITC

Detection:

- Identical quantities moving in loops
- No stock variation

Outcome:

- ITC disallowed
- Network dismantled
- **Case Study 7:** Real Enforcement Example – DGGI Crackdown

Agency Involved: Directorate General of GST Intelligence

Facts:

DGGI uncovered multiple nationwide fake ITC rackets involving thousands of shell firms.

Key Findings:

Fake ITC frauds exceeding ₹10,000 crore (across multiple operations)

- Use of professionals and intermediaries
- PAN-based identity misuse

Action Taken:

- Arrests across states
- Bank accounts frozen
- Large-scale GST registration cancellations

Key Lessons from These Cases

1. **Most GST frauds are ITC-driven**

- Fake invoices are the core mechanism
- No actual goods/services involved

2. **Data analytics is the biggest weapon**

- GSTN + e-way bill + banking data integration
- Pattern recognition (circular trading, fake firms)

3. **Common Red Flags**

- High ITC but low tax payment
- No physical infrastructure
- Repeated directors across firms
- Sudden spike in turnover

4. **Enforcement Strategy Shift**

Compared to old tax regimes:

- More technology-driven detection
- Faster arrests and prosecution

- Focus on network dismantling, not just individual firms

GST and Black Money

When GST was introduced, one of its unspoken promises was moral as much as economic: that a unified, digital tax would shrink the space for black money. Fewer taxes, fewer rates, one trail of invoices surely opacity would give way to transparency. Nearly a decade on, the picture is more complicated, and therefore more honest.

At the heart of GST lies a simple idea: every transaction should leave a digital footprint. Input Tax Credit (ITC) links the seller's tax payment to the buyer's tax claim, creating a chain of mutual verification. In theory, this makes it difficult to hide sales, suppress turnover, or operate entirely in cash.

GST also:

- Encouraged invoice-based accounting
- Nudged small businesses towards banking and digital payments
- Brought large parts of the informal supply chain into formal reporting

In sectors where invoices were earlier optional, they suddenly became essential.

Where GST Has Clearly Helped

There is little doubt that GST has reduced casual invisibility.

- Large and medium businesses now operate under continuous digital scrutiny
- Fake expenses and inflated purchases are harder to sustain
- Inter-state trade has become more traceable

- Shell entities face higher risk due to invoice matching and data analytics

Black money today finds it harder to hide in plain sight.

The Reality Check: Black Money Has Not Disappeared

Yet, black money has not vanished, it has adapted.

Cash transactions continue in:

- Small retail
- Real estate (especially land)
- Personal services
- Labour-intensive informal work

GST captures what enters the formal net. It does not automatically catch what stays outside it.

Moreover:

- Fake invoicing rackets have emerged
- ITC fraud has become a new frontier of tax evasion
- Compliance complexity has sometimes pushed smaller players back into cash dealings.

Digitisation alone does not eliminate intent.

Enforcement: Powerful, but Not Omnipresent

GST enforcement relies heavily on:

- Data analytics
- Invoice matching
- E-way bills
- Bank transaction intelligence

This makes the system strong against structured evasion, but weaker against fragmented, small-value cash transactions. Enforcement also depends on human discretion, where capacity, training, and integrity vary.

The law can demand compliance.

It cannot manufacture honesty.

Perhaps GST's greatest impact is not visible in seizure statistics but in behavioural change.

Businesses now think twice before:

- Suppressing turnover
- Issuing cash-only bills
- Maintaining dual accounts

The fear of digital trails has created a culture of partial compliance, which while imperfect is still progress.

Black money thrives on invisibility. GST has made invisibility expensive.

- What GST Cannot Do Alone
- GST is a tax system, not a moral cure.

It cannot:

- Replace income tax enforcement
- Eliminate political or real estate black money
- Fix weak prosecution or delayed adjudication
- Overcome social tolerance of cash dealings

Expecting GST to single-handedly eliminate black money is to misunderstand both black money and taxation.

GST has narrowed the space for black money, especially in organised commerce. It has not closed. Transparency has increased, but enforcement has limits. Digitisation has helped, but compliance fatigue is real.

The lesson is clear: systems deter, but values decide.

GST is a necessary weapon not a silver bullet.

High Court Quashed Cash Seizure:

The Bombay High court quashed the seizure orders

issued by the department and directed the return of Rs 1 crore in cash seized from Mumbai traders by the DGGI as perverse, arbitrary and without authority of law. The Hon'ble high court ruled that officers of the DGGI failed to comply with the statutory requirements under the GST law before seizing the money. The bench also expressed surprise when the government council informed the court that the seized cash had been handed over to the income tax department for further proceedings. The facts of the case are that the DGGI officers had seized Rs 60 lacs from the office premises and Rs 40 lacs from parents residence during search operation in connection with an investigation into an alleged fake input tax credit (ITC) racket involving another business man network of about 155 bogus firms was allegedly used to fraudulently avail and pass on ITC worth over Rs 3.8 crore without actual supply of goods. However the high court held that the seizure of cash did not satisfy the requirement of section 67(2) of the central goods and service tax act which empower officers to seize goods, documents, books are things only when there is reason to believe they are relevant to proceedings under the act. The bench noted that the department failed to record or demonstrate any such reason to believe in the impugned case.

Kar Vivad Samadhan Scheme

The Kar Vivad Samadhan Scheme, 1998 was a tax settlement initiative introduced in the 1998 Union Budget to allow taxpayers to settle disputed tax liabilities by paying a reduced amount and avoiding prolonged litigation.

The primary goal of the scheme was to provide a legal framework for settling tax disputes by offering partial waivers of unpaid taxes, penalties, and interest, along with immunity from prosecution for assessees (taxpayers) who opted in and withdrew their pending litigation. The scheme was open for declarations from September 1, 1998, to December 31, 1998 (later extended).

It covered tax arrears related to various direct and indirect tax enactments where an appeal, reference, or writ petition was pending before an appellate authority, High Court, or Supreme Court as of the date of the declaration.

Under the scheme:

Taxpayers could make a declaration of disputed tax arrears pending as of the cut-off date.

Once the settlement amount (a portion of the disputed tax) was paid, the case would be closed and the taxpayer would receive immunity from further civil proceedings or penalty on that issue.

Advantages:

1. **Faster settlement of disputes**

The scheme provided a mechanism to settle tax disputes without lengthy court battles, helping both taxpayers and tax authorities avoid protracted litigation.

2. **Reduced tax burden**

Taxpayers could pay a percentage of the disputed tax instead of the full amount effectively easing financial pressure compared to fighting a long dispute.

3. **Immunity from penalties and prosecution**

Once the settlement amount was paid under the scheme, the taxpayer was protected from penalties and further legal action on that matter, providing greater certainty.

4. **Encouraged revenue inflow**

The government could collect tax revenue sooner by resolving old disputes, rather than waiting years for litigation outcomes.

5. **Clarified procedural aspects**

Later clarifications ensured that settlement didn't prejudice taxpayers in future disputes on different years or matters improving fairness.

Disadvantages:

1. **Limited uptake historically**

Although the scheme was intended to solve many pending tax disputes, relatively few taxpayers opted in, meaning its impact was somewhat muted compared with later schemes like Vivad Se Vishwas.

2. **Only covers certain pending cases**

Eligibility was strictly based on whether tax arrears were determined and pending or already notified by a specific date, many disputes were excluded. This limited who could benefit.

3. **Partial benefit only**

The scheme did not eliminate all tax liabilities for many users; they still had to pay a share of the disputed amount. For some, this might still be significant or not worth opting in.

4. **Not a long-term solution**

Because it was a one-time special window, the scheme didn't establish an ongoing dispute resolution mechanism for disputes that arose after the cut-off had no similar relief. This reduced its utility over time.

5. **Interpretational and legal challenges**

Some aspects of the scheme's application led to court cases on interpretation, particularly around immunity and who benefits from the settlement showing that even settlement schemes can lead to further litigation.

Later schemes such as Vivad Se Vishwas (introduced in 2020 and updated in 2024) try to improve on Kar Vivad Samadhan by offering interest and penalty waivers, simpler processes, extended deadlines, and greater coverage of cases addressing some limitations of the older scheme.

Experts note that Vivad Se Vishwas has been more

successful than earlier initiatives, including Kar Vivad Samadhan, in both revenue collection and dispute resolution.

Sabka Vishwas (Legacy Dispute Resolution) Scheme, 2019:

The Sabka Vishwas (Legacy Dispute Resolution) Scheme, 2019 offered significant merits to taxpayers by providing a one-time opportunity to settle pending Central Excise and Service Tax disputes with substantial relief and immunity from prosecution. The Burden of the Past Large tax reforms do not merely create new systems; they inherit old disputes. The rollout of the Goods and Services Tax (GST) in July 2017 marked the most comprehensive overhaul of India's indirect tax architecture since Independence. Yet, even as GST promised simplicity and uniformity, the ghosts of the pre-GST regime Central Excise and Service Tax continued to haunt both taxpayers and the administration. The Sabka Vishwas (Legacy Dispute Resolution) Scheme, 2019 was not merely a fiscal measure; it was a symbolic closure of an era. By offering relief, finality, and immunity, it allowed both the State and the taxpayer to move forward without the weight of the past. In the long arc of India's tax reforms, Sabka Vishwas stands as an acknowledgment that efficient taxation is not only about collecting dues, but also about knowing when to settle, forgive, and close.

By 2019, lakhs of disputes involving thousands of crores of rupees were pending at various stages show cause notices awaiting adjudication, appeals stuck before Commissioners (Appeals), CESTAT, High Courts, and the Supreme Court. For taxpayers, these disputes represented uncertainty and blocked capital. For the government, they translated into stagnant revenue and mounting litigation costs. It was in this context that the Government of India introduced the Sabka Vishwas (Legacy Dispute Resolution) Scheme, 2019 (SVLDRS), a one-time legislative attempt to draw a definitive line under the pre-GST indirect tax era.

The Scheme was enacted through the Finance (No. 2) Act, 2019, not as a routine amnesty, but as a strategic litigation-management tool. Unlike earlier settlement schemes, Sabka Vishwas was consciously framed as a "legacy dispute resolution" mechanism, underscoring its limited temporal and substantive scope.

The philosophy was explicit:

- Revenue locked in litigation is not real revenue
- Prolonged disputes erode trust and compliance
- A modern tax system cannot be burdened by old law conflicts

The Scheme thus aligned with the broader policy shift towards:

- Non-adversarial tax administration
- Ease of doing business
- Trust-based compliance

Scope and Coverage of the Scheme

The Scheme applied exclusively to pre-GST central indirect taxes, including:

- Central Excise duty
- Service Tax under the Finance Act, 1994
- Allied cesses and surcharges subsumed under GST

Importantly, the cut-off date was **30 June 2019,** ensuring that only disputes genuinely rooted in the legacy regime were eligible.

Classification of Disputes: A Structured Approach

A key strength of SVLDRS lay in its granular categorisation of disputes, recognising that not all litigation stands on the same footing.

This included cases where:

- Appeals were pending before appellate authorities or courts
- Show cause notices had been issued but not finally adjudicated

Here, the dispute had already entered the formal adjudicatory ecosystem.

Arrears Category

Cases where:

- Tax dues had been confirmed
- Appeals were not filed or had attained finality

These represented enforceable but unrealised revenue.

Investigation, Enquiry, or Audit Category

Cases under:

- Ongoing investigation or audit

Provided the tax liability had been quantified on or before 30 June 2019

This condition ensured administrative certainty and prevented speculative declarations.

Voluntary Disclosure

Perhaps the most ethically charged category, voluntary disclosure allowed taxpayers to declare unpaid tax liability without any ongoing proceedings, offering waiver of interest and penalty, though no relief on tax amount.

Incentivising Closure

The Scheme offered significant relief on tax dues, calibrated to encourage early settlement while balancing revenue considerations.

- Up to 70% waiver in smaller disputes
- Up to 50% waiver in larger disputes

Complete immunity from:

- Interest
- Penalty
- Prosecution

Pre-deposits already made were adjusted against the final payable amount, though refunds were expressly barred reinforcing the Scheme's settlement-centric character.

The procedural architecture was deliberately kept digital, time-bound, and committee-driven.

- Declaration filed electronically
- Verification by a Designated Committee of officers
- Determination of payable amount
- Payment within stipulated time
- Issuance of a Discharge Certificate

The Discharge Certificate was the Scheme's most powerful instrument. Once issued, it:

- Conferred full and final settlement
- Barred reopening of the dispute
- Extinguished both departmental and taxpayer remedies.

To preserve credibility and prevent misuse, the Scheme excluded:

- Refund claims
- Erroneous refunds
- Cases involving prosecution or conviction
- Matters where liability was unquantified as of the cut-off date

These exclusions reflected a conscious effort to balance leniency with integrity.

From an institutional standpoint, Sabka Vishwas achieved outcomes that routine adjudication could not:

- Substantial reduction in litigation backlog
- Release of departmental resources from legacy cases
- Improved focus on GST compliance and enforcement
- Enhanced taxpayer confidence in consensual resolution

For courts and tribunals, the Scheme functioned as a pressure valve, easing docket congestion without judicial intervention.

Despite its success, the Scheme was not without criticism:

- Rigid timelines excluded some genuine cases
- No relief on tax under voluntary disclosure discouraged participation
- Absence of discretion in certain edge cases

Yet, these limitations were arguably inherent in any one-time, rules-based settlement framework.

Tax Treaties:

In a landmark judgment, the Supreme Court of India has fundamentally reshaped how international tax treaties apply to foreign investments into the country. How the legal interpretation of these investment vehicles has "changed its stripes" (changed its nature), prioritizing "economic substance" over legal form and reducing tax shield benefits?

In the case of Tiger Global International III Holdings vs. Authority for Advance Ruling, the apex court ruled that international tax treaties cannot be used as shields to avoid Indian taxes if the investment structure lacks genuine commercial substance.

The court's decision against Tiger Global in the sale of its Flipkart shares a transaction worth about ₹14,000 crore goes beyond settling a single tax dispute. It ends the long-standing assumption that simply holding a Tax Residency Certificate (TRC) alone is enough to claim tax benefits under Double Taxation Avoidance Agreements (DTAAs)

For years, many foreign investors routed capital through countries like Mauritius based on the belief that a TRC would prevent Indian taxation on capital gains. But in its recent ruling, the Supreme Court made it clear that a TRC by itself cannot indefinitely mask the true nature of a transaction or an investment structure. The court agreed with the tax authorities that Tiger Global's Mauritius entities were essentially pass-through conduits with no independent commercial operations or substance, used primarily to avoid tax. By setting aside the Delhi High Court's earlier order, the Supreme Court has emphasised that economic substance must prevail over mere legal form.

A particularly significant implication is the court's stance on grandfathering protections. Investments made before the 2017 amendment to the India-Mauritius tax treaty were widely thought to be permanently protected from Indian capital gains tax. However, the Supreme Court has suggested that even these protections cannot shelter arrangements that are essentially artificial or lacking substance.

Under this new approach, foreign investors now face a strict substance test. India's tax authorities can examine whether:

The holding company has real decision-making authority,

There is substantive economic activity in the treaty jurisdiction, and funds are genuinely invested rather than routed mechanically through conduit entities.

The ruling reflects a broader effort by India's judiciary to strike a balance: honour international tax treaty obligations, but not at the cost of India's fiscal sovereignty.

The message to global investors is clear tax benefits will be determined by commercial reality, not just paperwork.

As a result, the era of low-cost, tax-neutral routings through offshore jurisdictions with minimal substance is effectively coming to an end. Going forward, tax efficiency will require real operational substance and business activity, not just certificates or formal compliance.

Free Trade Accords

Indians have gone up living with the falsehood of international rule based order. New Delhi was the original middle power coalition builder. Reviving that project will be tough, but time for new global architecture has arrived. 'A moment comes, which comes but rarely in history, when we step out from the old to the new, when an age ends, and when the soul of a nation long suppressed finds utterance', these lines of Canadian PM, Mark Carney in Davos has woken to the real world who has risen from ashes of Bandug to a phoenix.

Hammer blows to multilateral trading systems have ushered in a new world, to which India is swiftly responding by shedding its earlier reputation for protectionism and trade diffidence. It has signed a raft of FTA culminating recently in the 'mother of all deals' with the EU. It has also reached an interim agreement with the US bringing down punitive tariffs but also committing India to eliminate or reduce tariffs on all US industrial goods and agricultural ones. Greater openness raises the economic stakes, giving rise to opportunity as well as risk. Being competitive is of existential importance for India industries and the economy. If we can maximise this can be another '1991' moment. Exports are essential for India's growth, and FTA are essential for a competitive shot of exports. A belief that India can't compete with other nations has cost it years of economic growth. While it will still not be able to win in all sectors, it needs to believe that it can dominate a few, overall India must target some FTA scale plays where it can win.

Rather than spreading itself too thin, India should pick 5-7 lines where it can be among the top three suppliers into partner markets, like textiles, garments, chemicals, auto components, pharma, electronics assembly and processed food. It should then streamline all elements that will make the sectors run smoothly, regulations, standard, testing labs, credit and logistic corridors. If India is still not able to compete in certain sectors despite a lower labour cost advantage of over 10 times compared with other countries, it has recently signed FTA with, then wisdom dictates those sectors should not be protected. Rather Indian consumers and producers should have access to the best product raw materials and capital goods and globally competitive prices. The biggest hidden risk in liberalisation and opening markets through FTA is transhipment from a country like China via the FTA route. China does enjoy a cost advantage over India in most categories magnified in many cases through mercantilist methods such as over capacity and dumping. In this case India's first line of defence must be data led rules of origin verification, risk scoring and penalties. Otherwise tariff cuts will become 'China plus one' via FTA. For India to fire on all cylinders of competitiveness it must also do everything possible to bring down input and factor costs for all sectors. In that sense, improved infrastructure, logistics and trade facilitations can be India's top export subsidy. Think rapid port turnaround, reduced customs dwell time, advanced inland logistics and paperwork digitalisation. These save costs for every sector without picking winners. India should use Vietnam as its benchmark and close specific gaps. This calls for some hard reforms to bring down factor cost, for instance, in power, land and capital going beyond the low hanging fruit that has already been picked. Vietnam 's secret sauce is policy consistency, trade facilitation and plugging into supply chains. India must replicate all this and focus on the boring fundamentals, stable and rationalised tariff policy, fast refunds, predictable compliance, and industrial clusters linked to ports /air cargo. Cheaper capital, a reliable power supply at competitive rates, greater scale and necessary skills. The practical package is a lower cost of credit for exporters, faster GST refund, easier availability of land and permits in export clusters and work force skilling tied to specific product lines, so that firms can scale before tariff walls come down fully. India has thoughtfully negotiated import tariffs that fall over time, instead of all at once. But time is short, this interval needs to be leveraged to the hilt for Indian industry to emerge fighting fit. Indian manufacturing has been stuck at around 16 -17% of GDP and its share of global manufacturing is around 2.8%, even as India has almost 20% of the world work force. This leaves close to half its work force trapped in less productive agriculture. Recent trade deals provide India with an opportunity to break out of this vicious cycle and trigger opportunity with both hands.

India has come a long way from the early days of its journey towards FTAs, which really began with an 'early harvest scheme' with Thailand that had limited coverage of under 100 products. The duty concessions meant that companies such as Honda and Sony began importing gear boxes and TV sets instead of producing them locally, putting the government on the defensive. What followed was a careful calibration with the government refusing to cut duties on sensitive sectors such as wine and spirits and automobiles. Things began to change with an interim deal with Australia in 2022, which followed India's decision to work out of Regional Comprehensive Economic Partnership (RCEP), the regional grouping led by China. For the first time, the government showed boldness in loading tariffs above specified value but sought to win over local producers by assuring technical support from their competitors. With every pact, the list got longer. So in came chocolates and watches in the pact with the European Free Trade Association comprising Switzerland, Norway, Iceland and Liechtenstein. Trade offs started going beyond goods and services. By the time the government finalized a list agreement with the EU, the eighth in 4 years, baring cereals, pulses, dairy products and genetically modified food, the red channel list became much shorter with Indian negotiatores learning to make trade offs. The modern FTAs include intellectual property rights, SMEs digital trade, labour and environment, but the commitments have not extended beyond what India has committed at international forums addressing concerns around patent laws being diluted. The entire world is looking at India's youth with a lot of trust and the reason behind that trust is skill and Sanskar.

Exports account for about 22% of India's GDP. Anything that enhances it, presents significant potential to boost domestic incomes and create employment. So far, India has been concluding trade agreements with individual countries- the UAE, Britain and New Zealand with the India- EU FTA it now steps into a larger stage. The EU offers unparalleled access to one of the world's most sophisticated markets. It is already India' s largest trading partner in goods in 2024-25, bilateral trade in goods reached $136.5 billion, while services trade crossed $83 billion. The largest FTA deepens this relationship by granting preferential market access to over 99% of Indian exports by value, across a combined economic space accounting for roughly a quarter of global GDP. It reaches 144 cr of India and 45 cr of EU total population. Official estimates suggest exports worth nearly $75 billion are now poised for accelerated growth, with labour intensive sectors set to gain significantly from immediate tariff elimination on nearly $ 33 billion of exports. These are not abstract gains. Export-led growth in these sectors supports large-scale employment particularly for women and semi skilled workers and strengthens regional manufacturing clusters across India. Preferential access combined with stronger regulatory cooperation and streamlined customs procedures under the FTA, can help these firms scale exports, invest with confidence and integrate more deeply into GVCs. The agreement also reflects calibrated trade-offs. India has agreed to a phased quota based liberalisation of automobile imports, while securing reciprocal access for India made vehicles in the EU. If managed well, this can strengthen ' make in India', enhance consumer choice and encourage tech transfer provided domestic manufacturing competitiveness continues to improve. Inclusion of forward looking CBAM provisions in the FTA covering dialogue, technical cooperation, recognition of carbon pricing mechanism and targeted support marks an important shift from unilateral regulation to structured engagement. This creates both challenge and opportunities for Indian industries. Carbon linked trade measures can raise near term compliance costs. But they also reward early movers in clean energy adoption and low carbon manufacturing. India has some of the world's lowest clean energy costs and highest availability. These position us well to compete in the emerging trade environment. The deal brings together advanced tech innovation and climate finance. While India offers scale manufacturing capabilities and a fast growing clean energy market. The larger market incentivised investment and partnership. India's demand for exemption from CBM must be understood in the context of a considerable financial, technological and capacity burden that aligning with EU climate norms would place on a large segment of industry particularly MSMEs. These are two economics with vastly different capacities. In 2025, the EU's nominal per capita GDP was about $46000, while India's was around $2800. The proposed EU- India platform for cooperation on climate action, to be set up by June, along with Euro 500 million in likely conditional EU support over the next 2 years will help. But it will clearly not suffice. However, just because CBAM feels unfair it doesn't mean it to be detrimental. New Delhi can turn it to its advantage. Talks on investment agreements should be approached with a clear sustainability lens and a concrete plan to decarbonise and transform the industrial base. The focus should be on attracting investments and partnership in clean energy supply chains, clean tech manufacturing and decarbonisation technology. Leveraging the complimentary of the two economies to create strategic opportunities that strengthen resilience and sustainability should be the guiding principles. If engaged proactively, CBAM could catalyse India's industrial transformation, rather than merely posing a constraint.

Further, a step change in EU India business partnerships in areas such as solar manufacturing, batteries, electric mobility, clean technology and semiconductors are also expected. This will help build resilient alternatives to concerned GVCs while supporting India's energy transition and job creation in future facing industries.

Growth spur if fixes in FTA are made. Textile exporters are at the forefront of beneficiaries from the India-EU trade deal. The relief comes at a challenging point for the industry which is facing a 50% tariff in the US, its biggest export market. The Government of India is opening labour intensive industry financial relief. But the US tariff action brought home the need to diversify it's exports in terms of export destinations. The obvious candidate, the EU previously had higher duty on textile imports from India which will now be brought to levels faced by principal competitors Bangladesh and Vietnam. Tariff equalization in the EU was a tough but necessary condition, the trade deal which was decades in the making, but several other hurdles confronted Indian exporters eyeing a larger share of the EU textile market. The main impediment is sustainability conditions imposed by the EU which will involve fresh investment by Indian exporters.

Investment will have to be made at all levels of the textile value chain, which would affect the competitiveness of MSMEs. The industry faces a supply chain that is fragmented across states and adds to logistics cost, unlike China, which has adopted an integrated approach to textile manufacturing. India also needs to make a bigger push into man made fibres, where taxes have kept input cost elevated. The EU trade deal may fall short of transforming India's textile industry into large manufacturing units unless supportive infrastructure and capitals are easier to access. The deal however offers the Indian textile industry a mechanism to transform technology and climb the value chain. Levelized tariffs are the starting point for a sustainable growth path. The industry is one of the biggest employment generators and primed for expansion through foreign investment. With access to the EU improving the growth trajectory, should shift upwards for India's textile sector. India must have an early harvest plan for EU textile exports and build on its inherent strength. The sector's linkages to agriculture contribute to its need for self-sustaining expansion.

This agreement, along with others like the India-UK FTA and the India-Australia ECTA, marks a strategic shift in India's trade policy focusing on deep market access while maintaining rigid safeguards for domestic sensitivity.

India's recent Free Trade Agreements (FTAs) especially with the European Union (EU) and other major partners like EFTA, the UK, Australia, and the UAE are beneficial to India across trade, investment, jobs, and strategic positioning. Their importance goes well beyond short-term tariff cuts. The recent wave of FTAs is designed to boost India's manufacturing, services, and export competitiveness: Under the India-EU FTA, nearly 90.7% of Indian exports (including textiles, leather, footwear, gems & jewelry, and marine products) will receive immediate duty-free access. This is expected to double exports in these sectors within a few years. India secured access to 144 EU service subsectors. Crucially, the deal includes a "Structured Mobility Framework" for short-term business travel and intra-corporate transfers, along with a commitment to discuss a Social Security Agreement within five years (which would prevent Indian professionals from losing social security contributions made abroad). Preferential access was gained for high-value items like tea, coffee, spices, fresh fruits (table grapes), and processed foods, which will directly boost rural incomes. The EU has pledged €500 million in support for India's green transition and established frameworks for cooperation in Artificial Intelligence (AI), semiconductors, and clean tech. While the potential gains from the India - EU FTA are evident, so too are the risks. It is hoped that the finalisation of FTA will galvanize the US into adopting a more flexible and pragmatic stance and concluding a trade deal with India at the earliest.

India's jewellery exports are pushing their way into the branded segment as the industry moves towards formalization. India is the world's largest exporter of jewellery. Yet, there is ample scope to climb up the value chain. The capitalisation funnel for the India jewellery industry has widened in recent years with interest by large business grow ups. This is aiding modernisation of the industry across the value chain from its import to re export. Quality assurance and design capabilities are giving branded jewellery the edge among India's growing middle class consumers with spill over effects on exports. Owners of leading brands are acquiring foreign brands to widen its footprint in West Asia while catering to regional design and brand sensitivity. Their showcase events in US and Europe are pitching a new design aesthetic in a crowded market. The international jewellery market is going through a rapid transformation, with demand for diamonds slaking due to laboratory grown varieties and a spike in bullion prices on account of heightened geopolitical uncertainty. Establishing brand presence in this scenario involves extra emphasis on aesthetic value. Europe offers some support for Indian jewellery exporters battered by the blink of Trump's tariff in the US, a big market after China and India. The trade deal with the EU will provide greater access for Indian jewellery exporters, provided they can negotiate the block sustainability requirements. Yet the need for diversification has become amply evident in the emerging global trade scenario. India has an advantage in the luxury segment of the jewellery business. More Indian brands are needed on the international stage to enforce the country's comparative advantage and jewellery exports. The design ecosystem must become much more robust for Indian artisanship to receive its dew recognition.

India's tariff concessions in the automobile and auto component sector especially the quota of 250,000 vehicles at low tariffs have raised concerns .While the government has clarified that the quota and duties have been carefully calibrated and low tariffs will become operational only after a few years, only specific details of the quota particularly for the buoyant electric vehicle sector can put doubt at rest. Also, according to the EU, India has committed to bringing tariffs on car parts to 0 over 5 - 10 years. It is uncertain whether our vibrant auto components industry will be able to face import competition under a tariff free regime. The dip in share price of auto majors after the FTA announcement reflected apprehension about the deal's impact on a critical segment of Indian manufacturing.

Consider how India's economy is to take advantage of these deals. In recent years cars, especially SUV, sales, domestic air passenger traffic, services exports and digital transactions have all passed record milestones. India's world class financial inclusion architecture helped lift nearly 270 million people out of extreme property in the past decade. India is also moving from assembly to invention, and securing resources, thereby deepening its role in global supply chains. Manufacturing clusters for vital components are emerging. New semiconductor facilities will advance materials research and produce IP. The defence corridors will make India self-reliant in research and manufacturing. And India's strategic needs will be met by a new rare earth corridor that was announced in the latest union budget. Today, products from those advanced manufacturing lines have tripled. For example,high end mobile phone manufacturing has grown so rapidly that India's mobile phone exports to the US have already surpassed China's in recent quarters. Similarly chip designs that originate at Indian design centres constitute about 20% of the world's capabilities. India dominates the specific niche of design verification, rigorous testing of chip's blueprint before it is manufactured. This process hinges on labour and proficiency and is vital to next generation smartphones, data centre and 5G infrastructure.

In AI too, India is well placed to lead. It has embraced AI faster and more comprehensively than any other nation. Voice, not text has emerged as the dominant mode of interaction with AI tools, allowing users to leap over literacy hurdles. There are over 700 million weekly active users of chatGPT globally, and India is the second largest market by usage for Open AI. About 92% of Indian office workers use AI tools regularly compared with 64% in the US. There is already a clear focus on developing indigenous AI tools at extremely low cost. Effects of the various deals, agreements and frameworks will take time to be felt. But, for now there is optimism that new possibilities are emerging from trade corridors in West Asia and digital embassies to green energy partnership and the new market for gas.

FTA and Press Note 3:

Press Note 3 (2020) is an Indian regulation that mandates prior government approval for any Foreign Direct Investment (FDI) originating from countries that share a land border with India (China, Pakistan, Bangladesh, Nepal, Myanmar, Bhutan, and Afghanistan).

It has been issued to prevent "opportunistic takeovers" of Indian companies during the COVID-19 pandemic. In practice, it most heavily impacts investments from China. While FTAs are designed to boost the exchange of goods and services. However, modern trade often requires "Investment-Led Trade." For example, if an Indian company wants to export high-tech electronics under a trade agreement, it might need to form a Joint Venture (JV) with a Chinese component manufacturer. The FTA encourages the trade of the finished product, but PN3 can delay or block the investment needed to build the factory in India to make that product. Most FTAs today focus on integrating countries into Global Value Chains.

Many global companies (even those from the US or Europe) have "beneficial owners" or supply chain partners in China. Until recently, PN3 was so broad that even a tiny Chinese stake in a European company could trigger a long approval process, effectively neutralizing the "ease of business" promised by trade accords with those regions.

As of March 10, 2026, the Indian government has relaxed PN3 to better align with its trade and manufacturing goals:

Investments where the "Beneficial Owner" from a land-bordering country holds less than 10% and has no management control can now go through the automatic route. For specific sectors like solar cells, electronic components, and capital goods, the government has introduced a 60-day deadline for PN3 clearances. This is intended to help Indian firms utilize trade agreements more effectively by getting the necessary technology and capital faster.

In the electronics and green energy sectors, Press Note 3 (PN3) historically acted as a major bottleneck because these industries are heavily dependent on Chinese components and expertise. However, as of March 10, 2026, the Indian government has pivoted from a "blanket ban" to a "surgical facilitation" approach to help these specific sectors grow.

1. Impact on the Electronics Sector

India's goal is to become a global electronics hub, but the sector faced a "Catch-22": it needed Chinese technology to build factories, but PN3 blocked the necessary investment.

India excels at final assembly (e.g., smartphones) but has "virtually no background" in making the actual components (PCBs, connectors, etc.). The government has now fast-tracked approvals for electronic components and "electronic capital goods" (the machinery needed to make electronics).

Instead of waiting 12–18 months, joint ventures (JVs) in electronics now get a decision within 60 days. Importantly, semiconductors remain under strict PN3 scrutiny. The government still views chips as too high-risk for foreign (Chinese) influence.

2. Impact on Green Energy

The relationship here is even more critical because China controls over 80% of the global supply chain for solar and EV batteries.

To meet climate goals, India needs to manufacture solar cells locally. PN3 previously stalled investments in the "upstream" part of the chain. The 2026 update specifically eases FDI for Polysilicon and Ingot-Wafers, the raw materials for solar panels. The new rules prioritize investments in Advanced Battery Components and Rare Earth Processing.

Indian firms like Dixon or Kaynes can now more easily partner with global tech leaders who might have small Chinese stakes (up to 10%) without needing a year of government paperwork.

Role of GST in the success of FTA:

The Goods and Services Tax (GST) acts as a

structural backbone for India's Free Trade Agreements (FTAs), particularly with sophisticated markets like the EU, UK, and Australia. By harmonizing the domestic tax landscape, GST removes the friction that previously made Indian exports less competitive. GST (Goods and Services Tax) can play a quiet but decisive role in ensuring that India actually benefits from Free Trade Agreements (FTAs) with the EU and other partners beyond just signing them. FTAs open doors; GST determines how well Indian firms can walk through them. GST directly contributes to the success of current FTA deals:

FTAs create opportunities; GST determines outcomes. GST helps India succeed in FTAs by:

- Making exports tax-neutral and competitive
- Proving origin and value addition
- Reducing logistics costs
- Formalising firms for global competition
- Aligning India with global VAT systems
- Protecting revenue while liberalising trade

In short, GST is India's domestic enabler of global integration. Without a robust GST, FTAs risk becoming paper agreements; with it, they can translate into sustained export growth, investment inflows, and global value-chain participation.

1. Zero-Rating of Exports

Under GST, exports are treated as "zero-rated supplies." This means that while no tax is levied on the final product sold to a foreign buyer, the exporter can still claim a refund for all taxes paid on inputs (raw materials, services, etc.). This ensures that India "exports goods, not taxes," keeping the final price low. In the newly signed India-EU FTA (Jan 2026), this allows Indian labor-intensive sectors like textiles and leather to fully capitalize on the zero-duty access granted by the EU. No GST is embedded in export prices

Exporters can claim refunds of input taxes

This aligns perfectly with FTA commitments, where price competitiveness is critical. For markets like the EU where margins are tight and compliance is strict, GST helps Indian exporters compete on real costs, not tax-loaded prices. Preferential tariffs under FTAs only help if Indian goods are competitively priced. GST ensures tax neutrality, allowing tariff benefits to translate into actual market gains.

2. **Elimination of the "Cascading Effect"**

Before GST, multiple layers of state and central taxes (VAT, Excise, Octroi) would "stack" on top of each other, leading to tax on tax. GST's Input Tax Credit (ITC) mechanism ensures that tax is paid only on the value added at each stage. This significantly lowers the cost of production, making Indian goods more price-competitive against global rivals like Vietnam or Bangladesh in FTA markets.

3. **Streamlined Logistics and Supply Chains**

The removal of inter-state check posts and the implementation of the E-way bill system have reduced transit times by an estimated 20–30%.

Modern FTAs emphasize "Ease of Doing Business." A faster domestic supply chain allows Indian manufacturers to meet the strict "just-in-time" delivery requirements of European and Western retail chains.

GST has:

- Removed inter-state tax barriers
- Reduced check-post delays
- Enabled integrated supply chains

This lowers:

- Inventory holding costs

- Transport time
- Compliance friction

When tariff barriers fall under FTAs, non-tariff costs (logistics, paperwork, delays) become decisive. GST improves India's ranking on these hidden cost parameters.

4. Simplified "Rules of Origin" Compliance

FTAs require strict "Rules of Origin" to ensure that only goods truly made in India benefit from lower tariffs. The digital nature of GST provides a transparent, verifiable trail of every transaction and input used in a product. This high level of documentation makes it easier for Indian exporters to prove domestic value addition during audits by foreign customs authorities. FTAs (especially with the EU) rely heavily on Rules of Origin (RoO) to prevent trans-shipment via third countries.

GST helps by:

- Creating a digitally traceable tax chain
- Recording value addition at each stage
- Offering invoice-level transparency

This makes it easier for Indian exporters to prove domestic value addition, a key requirement for claiming FTA benefits.

The EU applies some of the world's strictest origin verification norms. GST's audit trail strengthens India's credibility in meeting them.

5. Level Playing Field for Imports (IGST)

When goods are imported

***

Politics, Proximity, and Pressure

Politics enters the Indian Revenue Service long before it announces itself.It arrives not as instruction, but as atmosphere. Not as command, but as proximity. By the time an officer learns to recognise it, its influence has already been absorbed into routine.

Unlike other pressures, political pressure rarely demands illegality. It demands timing, restraint, and silence. It works best when it appears unnecessary.

Every posting has a geography.Some offices are distant from political centres, insulated by routine and remoteness. Others sit close to power not always physically, but functionally. Files from these offices travel faster, attract more attention, and acquire meanings beyond their contents.

An officer soon realises that where you sit matters as much as what you do.

In such locations, political awareness becomes a survival skill. Not allegiance, not obedience but understanding. Understanding when a file is merely administrative, and when it has crossed into the political bloodstream.

No circular teaches this. It is learned by watching which files move smoothly, which hesitate, and which return with no comment but altered expectations.

Proximity Without Contact

Most political pressure is indirect.

Few officers receive explicit calls from politicians.

Those who do rarely forget it.

But these are exceptions. The more common form is subtler messages relayed through intermediaries, questions asked in meetings without attribution, hints dropped without ownership. An officer may be asked whether a particular case is "sensitive." Or whether a notice "needs urgency." Or whether discretion is "available."Each question is deniable. Each places the burden of interpretation on the officer. The genius and cruelty of this system is that no one needs to issue an order. The officer is expected to anticipate alignment.

Timing as Pressure Politics is impatient.

Files that coincide with elections, budgets, alliances, or crises acquire a sensitivity unrelated to law. An action taken today may be welcomed; the same action taken tomorrow may be condemned. Officers learn that timing is not neutral. Enforcement at the wrong moment becomes provocation. Delay at the right moment becomes wisdom. This temporal sensitivity is rarely articulated, yet widely understood.It forces officers to confront an uncomfortable question: Is postponement prudence or complicity?

There is no universal answer. Only context.

The Borrowed Authority of Name

A file attached to an unknown entity is administrative. The same file, once associated accurately or otherwise with a political figure, becomes radioactive.

Often, the association is indirect: a relative, a donor, a former associate. Legally irrelevant, but institutionally potent.

Once a name enters conversation, the tone changes. Discussions become cautious. Advice becomes conditional. Silence grows thicker.

The officer realises that political power does not need to intervene; it merely needs to be present in imagination.

The Myth of Resistance

Popular narratives celebrate officers who "stood up to politicians. "Reality is less dramatic, more ambiguous.

Resistance is rarely heroic. It is procedural. It involves insisting on written communication, recording reasons carefully, refusing urgency without explanation, slowing down without stalling.

Open confrontation is almost always counterproductive. It creates spectacle, invites retaliation, and isolates the officer.

The most effective resistance is invisible so thoroughly embedded in the process that it appears natural. But invisibility has its price: no recognition, no vindication, only the quiet knowledge that you did not bend.

Transfers as Language

In the IRS, transfers speak louder than instructions. A sudden posting change following an inconvenient decision is rarely explained. It does not need to be. The message is understood not just by the officer transferred, but by those watching. These moves are not always punitive. They are illustrative. The system rarely disciplines openly. It educates through example.

Young officers absorb these lessons quickly. Some become cautious. Others become compliant. A few become indifferent, treating postings as fate rather than feedback.

Political Neutrality as Daily Labour

Neutrality is not a state; it is a practice.

It requires constant adjustment engaging without aligning, hearing without agreeing, responding without committing. It is emotionally exhausting. Officers must often act in ways that appear inconsistent: firm in one case, restrained in another; decisive here, patient there. From outside, this looks arbitrary. From inside, it is calibration.

Mistakes are inevitable. Misjudgments frequent.

What sustains neutrality is not purity, but consistency of reasoning the ability to explain, on paper and later, why a particular course was chosen.When Pressure Crosses the Line Occasionally, pressure becomes explicit.

A call is made. A message conveyed. A request framed as advice but heard as expectation.These moments are rare, but decisive. The officer stands at a fork: comply, resist, or deflect. Compliance may solve the immediate problem but creates precedent. Resistance may protect integrity but invite consequences. Deflection buys time, not resolution. No option is clean. The service does not offer protection in advance, only evaluation in hindsight. Many officers discover here that courage is not rewarded immediately, but compromise is remembered quickly.

The Personal Cost

Political pressure does not end at office doors.

It seeps into family conversations, social circles, and self-perception. Officers become guarded in public, vague in private. Friendships are thin. Trust becomes selective.

This isolation is rarely acknowledged. The public sees power; the officer experiences exposure. Some retreat inward. Others grow cynical. A few develop a detached professionalism that shields without hardening.

Politics reveals the service to itself.

It exposes which safeguards work and which exist only on paper. It tests the strength of institutions and the endurance of individuals.

Most of all, it reveals that the greatest pressure on an IRS officer is not to act illegally, but to act inconspicuously when legality becomes inconvenient.How one responds to that pressure shapes not only career, but character.

The officer does not emerge victorious or defeated. He emerges aware, aware that power has many centres, that pressure is rarely singular, and that neutrality is fragile but necessary.

***

Corruption, Temptation, and Vigilance

Corruption in the Indian Revenue Service is rarely loud. When it is loud, it is quickly discovered. When it is quiet, it survives.

The popular imagination treats corruption as a moral failure, an individual choosing greed over duty. The reality is more complex, less theatrical, and therefore more dangerous. Corruption often begins not with intent, but with erosion.

The Proximity of Temptation

Few services place officers so close to wealth.

Every day, IRS officers encounter figures that dwarf their own salaries transactions that compress years of income into single entries. They deal with businesses that survive by negotiation, not compliance; with intermediaries skilled in suggestion rather than request.

Temptation does not arrive as a suitcase of cash. It arrives as a convenience.

A representative offers to "resolve matters." A taxpayer hints at gratitude. A middleman speaks of mutual benefit without naming it. Each interaction is calibrated to be deniable.

The officer's first defence is clarity. The second is distance. Lose either, and the line blurs quickly.

The Normalisation of Small Deviations

Corruption rarely begins with large decisions.

It begins with silence where explanation was due. With delay instead of decision. With selective urgency. With overlooking what could have been pursued. These actions do not feel corrupt. They feel practical. An officer tells himself he is avoiding unnecessary conflict. Preserving institutional harmony. Choosing battles wisely. Each justification is plausible. Each step is small.

Over time, however, the cumulative effect becomes unmistakable. The officer no longer decides based on law alone, but on convenience, comfort, and consequence.

This is how erosion occurs not by collapse, but by accommodation.

The Marketplace Around the Service

Corruption thrives not only because officers err, but because an ecosystem exists to enable error. Chartered accountants, consultants, fixers, retired officials some honest, some not operate at the periphery of the service. They understand the procedure intimately. They know where discretion lies and where pressure works.

They speak the language of plausibility.

An officer who believes himself immune often underestimates this ecosystem. Corruption does not require coercion. It requires familiarity.

Why Some Fall and Others Do Not

Not all officers succumb. Many do not.

The difference is not virtue alone. It is context, temperament, and fatigue.

Officers under constant pressure, isolation, or frustration are more vulnerable. Those who feel unrewarded, unprotected, or invisible may begin to rationalise. Those who believe the system is unfair may decide to extract fairness privately.

None of this excuses misconduct. But understanding it explains why vigilance must be institutional, not moralistic.

Vigilance: The System Watching Itself

Vigilance exists because trust is insufficient.

The Central Vigilance Commission, internal vigilance units, and investigative agencies form a lattice of oversight designed to detect deviation. Their presence is necessary, but their reach is imperfect.Vigilance rarely discovers corruption at its inception. It discovers patterns assets disproportionate to income, complaints repeated, decisions clustered suspiciously.

By the time vigilance notices, the damage is usually done. This delay creates fear among honest officers and overconfidence among dishonest ones.

Fear and the Honest Officer

Vigilance does not distinguish intent easily.

An honest mistake, poorly documented, can invite the same scrutiny as deliberate wrongdoing. This equivalence breeds fear.

Officers begin to write defensively, decide cautiously, and avoid complexity. Some prefer inaction to initiative, believing that a delayed file is safer than a decided one.

This culture of fear is corrosive. It protects the cautious, not the correct. It rewards invisibility over integrity.

And yet, without vigilance, corruption flourishes openly.

The service lives in this paradox.

When Vigilance Becomes Personal

Most officers encounter vigilance not as an investigation, but as a possibility.

A file is called for. A clarification sought. An anonymous complaint forwarded. The language is neutral; the impact is not.

Sleep becomes lighter. Memory is unreliable. One replays decisions repeatedly, searching for omissions, misinterpretations, unrecorded conversations.

Often, the matter ends quietly. But the experience leaves residue.

Officers learn that vigilance is not an event, but a condition of constant background presence that shapes behaviour.

The Myth of Zero Tolerance

Official discourse speaks of zero tolerance.

Reality is messier.The system punishes visible corruption more readily than subtle compromise. It is easier to prosecute acceptance of bribes than patterns of selective enforcement. Some officers are caught. Others retire quietly. Many operate in grey zones that never trigger thresholds. This unevenness fuels cynicism among the honest and arrogance among the corrupt.

Every officer draws a line.For some, it is absolutely no accommodation, no favour, no deviation. For others, it is conditional no money, but procedural flexibility. For a few, the line shifts until it disappears.

The tragedy is not that lines exist, but that they are drawn privately, without collective reinforcement.

Institutions fail when ethics become individual rather than shared.

Integrity Without Romance

Integrity in the IRS is unglamorous.

It does not protect you from pressure. It does not guarantee good postings. It does not ensure appreciation. Often, it complicates life.

What it offers instead is continuity the ability to look back without flinching.

For many officers, that is enough. For others, it is insufficient.

The service accommodates both, uneasily.

Corruption teaches officers uncomfortable truths. That temptation is ordinary. That system is porous. That morality is not static. That vigilance, while necessary, is blunt.

Most of all, it teaches that the battle against corruption is not fought in dramatic confrontations, but in daily decisions that no one notices. The Indian Revenue Service is neither uniquely corrupt nor exceptionally virtuous. It is human, operating under extraordinary authority with ordinary safeguards.But no system can eliminate choice. And where choice remains, so does temptation.

Let us come to tax policies that boost smuggling. Trump's attack on the dollar is fueling the rise of gold. That, in tandem with India's high import duty on gold, makes gold smuggling even more attractive. Dump that duty, bring it down to 2%, the level in 2012. Criminality that attends on smuggling corrupt swaths of public life.

The recently proposed excise and GST hike on cigarettes of effective 70% duty, promise vastly increased smuggling of cigarettes. Conversion of smuggled gold into jewellery creates jobs in India. But smuggled cigarettes displace domestic cigarettes. Jobs and income are lost in the domestic cigarette industry and tobacco farming. Once the smuggling and distribution network for cigarettes is established, it gets entrenched. The effect of sin tax on cigarettes sold in the country are smuggled, bearing no tax, other than the bribes that grease their path, deprive Government of India revenue and blunt the tax sting altogether. Higher the sin tax, cheaper the cigarettes on the market, and greater the sin.

Corruption is often described as a "structural cancer"

because it does not merely divert financial resources; it progressively erodes the institutions designed to serve and protect the public. It is not just a moral failing, but a systemic risk factor that undermines governance efficiency, economic growth, institutional legitimacy, and social equity.

Its severity depends on three core variables: scale, normalization, and enforcement gaps. In many developing systems, including India, corruption is best understood not as a binary phenomenon but as a spectrum problem, ranging from petty facilitation payments to deeply embedded systemic distortions.

At a functional level, corruption imposes direct costs on citizens and small businesses, normalizes illegality, and distorts administrative processes. In India, for example, GST frauds (such as fake invoicing and ITC manipulation) illustrate how corruption increasingly overlaps with organized financial crime. Similarly, leakages in public procurement significantly inflate project costs. Corruption is therefore best viewed as a chronic institutional disease often invisible, but continuously degrading system performance unless actively countered through transparency, enforcement, and simplification.

One of its most severe dimensions is normalization. When corruption becomes embedded in routine transactions, it ceases to be perceived as deviant behavior and instead becomes a "cost of doing business." Breaking this cycle requires not only legal reform but also structural transparency and robust digital systems that minimize discretionary human intervention.

Analytical Framework: What Drives Corruption

At its core, corruption is the abuse of entrusted power for private gain. It typically arises when three elements converge:

- Power or authority (e.g., public officials, corporate decision-makers)
- Discretion (the ability to make subjective decisions)
- Weak accountability or transparency

When these conditions coexist, the probability of corruption increases significantly.

Corruption operates not randomly, but as a system of incentives and networks, typically following a predictable pattern:

Opportunity emerges (e.g., contract award, tax assessment, permit approval)

Discretion is exercised in an environment of weak enforcement

An informal "price" is negotiated (bribe, favor, political support)

Exchange occurs (money, influence, or benefits)

Cover-up mechanisms are activated (fake documentation, shell entities, delays)

Gains are distributed across a network (officials, intermediaries, political actors)

Types of Corruption

- **Petty Corruption:** Small bribes for routine services (e.g., permits, fines).
- **Grand Corruption:** Large-scale manipulation of policies or contracts (e.g., infrastructure, defense deals).
- **Systemic Corruption:** Embedded within institutions, where rules exist but are routinely bypassed.

Systemic corruption is the most damaging, as it distorts markets, reduces trust, and entrenches inequality.

Measuring the Severity of Corruption

1. **Economic Impact**

Corruption acts as a hidden tax on the economy:

- Discourages Foreign Direct Investment due to unpredictability
- Causes resource misallocation, diverting funds to low-value or "kickback-friendly" projects
- Distorts markets by rewarding connections over competence

2. **Erosion of Social Justice**

The burden is disproportionately borne by the poor:

- Access to healthcare, education, and welfare becomes conditional on informal payments.
- Wealth concentrates among elites, widening inequality and social tensions.

In philosophical terms, corruption represents a return to a state of anarchy often described as Matsya Nyaya where the big fish eat the small fish.

The Moral Failure: Ethics and "Dharma" are meant to protect the vulnerable. Corruption reverses this, allowing those with wealth and power to exploit those without it, effectively replacing the "rule of law" with the "rule of might

3. **Institutional and Political Decay**

Corruption undermines the social contract:

- Erodes trust in institutions such as the police, judiciary, and political system
- Weakens the rule of law, creating environments where power overrides legality

Corruption in India's GST System

The Goods and Services Tax (GST) was designed as a digital, rule-based, and "contactless" system to reduce human intervention. However, corruption persists at points of discretionary authority.

Key Vulnerability: "Human Intervention Points"

1. **Registration Stage**

- Officials may raise technical objections and delay approvals
- Informal payments are sometimes solicited to "move files faster"
- Root causes: discretionary verification and weak enforcement of timelines

Corruption in GST Refunds: How It Manifests

Although GST refunds are partially automated, corruption emerges at verification and approval stages.

Entry Points in the Refund Pipeline

- Filing on GST portal
- System validation
- Officer scrutiny (critical risk point)
- Refund approval
- Common Mechanisms

A. **Speed Money for Refund Clearance**

Deliberate delays create pressure on businesses (especially MSMEs), leading to informal payments to expedite refunds.

B. **Artificial Objections**

Minor discrepancies are raised repeatedly to:

- Prolong the process
- Create negotiation leverage

C. **Discretion in Risk Flags**

"Risky exporter" classifications involve human interpretation, creating high-value corruption nodes.

D. Collusion in Fraudulent Refunds

Officials may knowingly approve fake ITC-based refund claims, transforming corruption into organized crime.

E. Manipulation of Verification Reports

Discrepancies may be exaggerated (to extract bribes) or ignored (to facilitate fraud).

F. Use of Intermediaries

Consultants and brokers act as intermediaries, quoting "rates" (often 1–5% of refund value), reducing traceability.

Structural Drivers of GST Corruption

- **Partial Automation:** Filing is digital, but decisions remain discretionary.
- **Working Capital Pressure:** Businesses depend heavily on timely refunds.
- **Legal Complexity:** Ambiguities in classification and ITC eligibility create grey areas.
- **Weak Accountability:** Limited consequences for delays or arbitrary decisions.

GST Fraud Ecosystem in India

Common Fraud Patterns

- **Fake ITC Chains:** Networks of shell firms generate bogus invoices to claim refunds
- **Missing Traders:** Entities vanish after issuing invoices without paying tax
- **Export Overvaluation:** Inflated invoices to claim higher refunds
- **Inverted Duty Abuse:** Inflated input purchases to maximize ITC refunds

- **E-way Bill Manipulation:** Fake logistics trails to support fraudulent transactions
- **Professional Syndicates:** Organized networks involving consultants and layered financial structures

Detection Framework Used by Authorities

Enforcement agencies use data-driven intelligence models:

- Data triangulation across GST, customs, banking, and income tax systems.
- Network analytics to detect circular trading patterns
- Risk scoring algorithms based on anomalies (e.g., high ITC vs low tax payment).
- Supplier chain verification to identify breaks in tax payment.
- Logistics validation using e-way bills and transport data.
- Banking analysis to trace fund flows.
- Physical verification of business premises.
- Identity linkage analysis (common IPs, directors, contact details).
- Customs-GST integration for export fraud detection
- Enforcement actions (arrests, asset attachment, cancellations).

Persistent Challenges

- **Speed vs accuracy trade-off:** Fraud often detected after refunds are issued
- **Residual human discretion:** Key decisions remain non-automated
- **Legal complexity in prosecution:** Difficult to prove intent.

- **Scale of data:** Millions of transactions complicate real-time monitoring.

Corruption in GST is not random, it emerges where three factors intersect:

- Discretion + Delay + Dependency
- Discretion creates authority
- Delay creates leverage

Dependency creates vulnerability

Unless these are structurally minimized through true rule-based automation, transparency, and strict accountability corruption will persist, even if its form evolves from petty bribery to sophisticated financial crime.

Dr Awdhesh Singh, Director Awadhesh Academy reports in Quora, facebook,corruption in a tax department is directly proportion to the tax evasion. If businessmen can't evade taxes, they would also not bribe the tax officials for corrupt practices. The Goods and Services Tax (GST) is an attempt by the Government to tax all activities relating to supply of goods and services.Despite the transformative potential of the Goods and Services Tax (GST) regime, corruption within its administration continues to undermine its credibility, efficiency, and the ease of doing business. If GOI really wants reforms, it has to clean up its internal act. The corruption is likely to be reduced for the following reasons.

Reduced Net Taxes

The taxpayers shall be eligible to take credit of the taxes on all the inputs across India, which would reduce his net tax liability. Let a manufacturer of an item of Rs 100 using the inputs of Rs 80 purchased from different tax payers. Let the rate of GST be 20%. In the present regime taxes of 20% of Rs 100 i.e. Rs 20; is paid, if he is purchasing all your inputs without bills. If only a few inputs, around 50% of your inputs suffer tax, he gets credit of the taxes on the inputs used. This is calculated to be 50% of Rs 80 i.e. on Rs 40 @20% viz. Rs 8. Hence total tax liability is Rs 20- Rs 8 = Rs 12

In the GST regime all goods and services would be taxed. Hence, he would get credit @20% on Rs 80 i.e. Rs 16 and his net tax liability would be Rs 4 only. Hence, his net liability reduced from Rs 20 without bills to Rs 12 with 50% bills to Rs 4 in GST regime; even though the tax rates remained the same. Thus, the net tax rate to an honest taxpayer is just 4% of Rs 100 in the GST regime with the GST rate at 20%. Hence, there would be less incentive to evade taxes now when the effective GST rate is just 4%. It is so because, if he is caught by tax authorities, he has to pay Rs 20 as GST (without credit) plus Rs 20 as penalty. Most taxpayers would therefore avoid evasion in GST regime.

Reduced Interface

All the returns of the taxpayers shall be filed online in the GST regime. They would also get all their refunds, orders etc. online. This will reduce the interface between the assessees and officers, which would reduce corruption.

Greater Transparency

The GST Network (GSTN) is designed to capture all transaction details up to invoice level. Hence, you can't escape the inputs or services used in providing the goods or services. The paper documentations are to be eliminated completely. Your data would be visible to state as well as central government officers. It would be difficult to hide anything.

Dual Control

GST will be monitored jointly by Central and state government officials. It would be difficult to manage some officers and do evasions. The chances of getting caught would be double in the GST regime.

Hence, the GST regime is likely to improve tax compliance and reduce corruption.

The psychology of corruption is a complex interplay between individual moral reasoning, social environment, and the structural "rules of the game." It is rarely as simple as "good people" versus "bad people"; rather, it often involves rationalization and the erosion of ethical boundaries over time.

To understand why individuals engage in corrupt behavior, we can look at it through three primary lenses:

1. **The Individual Level: Rationalization and "Slippery Slopes"**

Most people who engage in corruption still view themselves as "good people." They achieve this through moral disengagement a process of convincing themselves that ethical standards do not apply to them in a specific context.

The Slippery Slope: Corruption often starts small. A minor, "harmless" favor sets a new baseline. Once that line is crossed, the next step feels less extreme, eventually leading to significant ethical breaches.

Rationalization Techniques:

- **Denial of Victim:** "No one is really getting hurt; it's just a big corporation/government."
- **Social Weighting:** "Everyone else is doing it, so I have to do it to stay competitive."

- **Metaphor of the Ledger:** "I've worked hard and been underpaid for years; I've earned this little extra."

2. **The Group Level: Normalization and Power**

The environment plays a massive role in shaping individual choices. If a culture treats corruption as a survival mechanism or a standard perk of a job, the psychological cost of participating drops significantly.

Social Normalization: When corruption becomes "the way things are done," it ceases to feel like a moral choice and starts feeling like a logistical one.

The Hubris Syndrome: High-stakes power can lead to a psychological state where an individual feels exempt from the rules. Power can diminish empathy and increase overconfidence, making the risk of being caught seem negligible.

3. **The Structural Level: The "Fraud Triangle"**

Criminologist Donald Cressey developed the Fraud Triangle, which explains the three factors that must be present for a person to commit a corrupt act:

- **Pressure:** A non-shareable financial problem or a high-stress desire to meet targets.
- **Opportunity:** A flaw in the system or a position of trust that allows the act to occur with low perceived risk of being caught.
- **Rationalization:** The internal justification that makes the act acceptable to the person's conscience.

Evolutionary Perspectives

Some psychologists argue that corruption stems from an ancient evolutionary drive: Kin Selection and Reciprocal Altruism. In our ancestral past, favoring your own "tribe" or family was a survival advantage. In a modern, merit-based society, this same impulse manifests as nepotism or cronyism. The psychological challenge is overriding these deep-seated tribal instincts in favor of abstract, large-scale systems like "the law" or "the public good."

Breaking the Cycle

Combatting the psychology of corruption requires more than just harsher punishments. It involves:

- **Increasing Transparency:** Reducing the "Opportunity" leg of the triangle.
- **Protecting Whistleblowers:** Changing the social cost of remaining silent.
- **Ethical Priming:** Regularly reminding individuals of their professional codes of conduct to prevent moral disengagement.

Managing Temptation and Strengthening Vigilance in GST Administration

Corruption in tax administration is not merely an ethical issue, it is a systemic risk arising from the interaction of:

- Human psychology (temptation, rationalization)
- Institutional design (discretion, opacity)
- Incentive structures (low detection probability, delayed punishment)

In the GST ecosystem, corruption typically manifests in:

- Fake Input Tax Credit (ITC) facilitation
- Fraudulent refund approvals
- Suppression or dilution of enforcement actions

The core challenge is not just detection of fraud, but preventing the conditions that enable temptation.

Temptation operates as a predictable behavioral mechanism:

- **Trigger:** Opportunity (e.g., discretionary approval power)
- **Desire:** Immediate personal gain
- **Rationalization:** "Low risk", "everyone does it"
- **Decision**: Influenced by detection risk and norms
- **Reinforcement:** Repetition builds habit and networks.
- **Temptation intensifies when:** Discretion is high and monitoring is weak. Consequences are uncertain. Thus, corruption control must shift from moral enforcement to system design.

A typical GST enforcement case follows a structured pipeline:

- **Trigger:** System analytics, intelligence, or field input
- **Preliminary scrutiny:** Desk-based risk validation
- **Case registration:** Formal investigation approval
- **Data mining:** Invoice chain and network mapping
- **Field verification:** Physical existence checks
- **Evidence collection:** Documents, returns, logistics
- **Statements:** Key persons examined
- **Money trail analysis:** Banking and fund flows
- **Quantification:** Tax evasion calculation
- **Legal framing:** Classification of offence
- **SCN issuance:** Evidence-backed legal notice

Adjudication & prosecution

- **Operational Reality:** Success depends on aligning: Invoice trail and Money trail. Physical non-existence

Failure Points in Enforcement

Cases often collapse due to: Weak evidence linkage,

Over-reliance on statements (later retracted), Inadequate field verification.

Failure to establish intent (mens rea)

This highlights the need for process rigor and documentation discipline.

Systemic Approach of Engineering Out Temptation-

Effective reform reduces both opportunity and payoff of corruption. Reduce Discretion Rule-based automated approvals (refunds, registration), System-driven scrutiny selection.

Limits negotiation space

Ensure End-to-End Digitization, Full audit trails of decisions.Timestamped officer actions Eliminates opacities.

- Strengthen Data Matching
- Invoice matching (Supplier–buyer)
- Integration with e-way bills and returns
- Makes fraud complex and traceable
- Risk-Based Enforcement
- AI/analytics-driven case selection
- Focus on high-probability fraud networks
- Reduces arbitrary targeting
- Segregation of Duties
- Separate roles for investigation, approval, and audit
- Increases coordination cost of corruption
- Real-Time Monitoring
- Dashboards tracking refunds and actions
- Early deviation detection
- Reduces delayed accountability
- Process Standardization

Uniform SOPs and documentation requirements. Minimizes interpretational ambiguity

Increase Probability of Detection

Data integration across agencies. Continuous analytics. Enhances deterrence more than punishment severity

Reduce Human Interface

- Faceless compliance systems
- Automated notices and communication
- Cuts rent-seeking points

5.10 Network-Level Enforcement

- Target entire fraud ecosystems (not individuals)
- Raises systemic risk for participants.

Continuous System Evolution

- Rapid policy and analytics updates
- Feedback-driven tightening
- Keeps pace with evolving fraud patterns

Strengthening Vigilance Framework

A robust vigilance system should operate across three layers:

Structural Controls -

- Minimize discretion via automation
- Standardize enforcement procedures
- Implement rotation policies in sensitive posts

Data Intelligence -

- Advanced analytics for anomaly detection
- Cross-agency data sharing (GST, Income Tax, FIU, Customs)
- Network analysis tools for fraud mapping

Accountability Mechanisms -

- Digital audit trails of officer actions
- Performance monitoring dashboards
- Time-bound processing with escalation triggers
- Independent vigilance audits

Strategic Shift: From Policing to Design -

- Traditional vigilance relies on post-facto detection and punishment.
- Modern systems must focus on:
- Prevention through design
- Real-time detection
- Certainty of accountability

Corruption declines when systems are structured such that: Wrongdoing is difficult to execute. Actions are fully visible and traceable and Detection is highly probable. Compliance is easier than violations.

Strengthening GST vigilance requires a transition from individual integrity-based control to system-driven governance architecture.

The objective is not merely to catch misconduct, but to reshape the incentive environment so that:

Honest behavior becomes the default, and corruption becomes operationally unviable.

Strength of Temptation

Only the living beings are tempted. A mountain is never tempted. A stone doesn't argue with itself. Temptation belongs exclusively to beings who can imagine another possibility. In that sense temptation is not merely a moral test, it is evidence of consciousness. The moment temptation appears a thought, a taste, a possibility the mind was not planning to entertain something, begins. Desire leans forward. Discipline clears its throat. Curiosity quietly takes notes.

The learned call this weakness but perhaps it is the opposite. Temptation is simply the mind discovering that the road has more than one direction. That is why our mythologies circle around temptation with almost ritual fascination. It appears temptation is the narrative engine of civilization, without it, most epics would end on page three. Yet, societies have always been wary of it. Order prefers predictable citizens. Temptation includes volatility, a person wrestling with temptation is thinking, weighing, questioning. Institutions prefer obedience. Temptation breeds reflection so temptation is vilified.

But look closely and the logic begins to wobble. Virtue itself depends on temptation. A monk renouncing the world must first feel the tug of the world. Patience is meaningless without impatience. Even restraint owes its existence to the patience of desire. Without temptation virtue would be unemployed. This is why temptation makes us weaker and stronger at the same time. When we yield, we encounter our fragility. When we resist, we discover our strength. Either way we learn something essential about the architecture of our mind. There is also a quiet hypocrisy in how societies speak about temptation. The same cultures that preach restraint have built magnificent industries around seduction. Markets tempt us hourly with brighter screens, sweeter flavours, faster pleasures. Advertising has become the organised science of temptation, conducted with algorithms instead of violins. Temptation is condemned in sermons and manufacturered in boardrooms. And then, when individuals stumble under this carefully engineered avalanche of desire, the blame returns politely to personal morality. Perhaps temptation has been misunderstood. Temptation is not merely a moral trap, it is a mirror. It reveals what we long for, what we fear and what we can refuse. Character does not grow in the absence of temptation, it grows in its shadow. The saint and the sinner are, in the sense cousins. Both have heard the same whisper, and that is quite a secret temptation carriage within it.

***

Ethics, Resilience, and Service Mindset

Taxation is critical for economic development, serving as the primary tool for governments to mobilize domestic resources, fund public infrastructure (roads, schools, healthcare), and reduce income inequality. It drives growth by funding investments, controls inflation through demand management, and influences economic behavior via targeted incentives.

Taxes provide essential funds for governments to invest in public goods and infrastructure, reducing dependence on external debt.

Progressive taxation (higher rates on higher incomes) helps redistribute wealth and improve social welfare by supporting public services for lower-income groups. By adjusting tax rates, governments can manage consumer demand to control inflation and stabilize the economy.

Investment and Growth Incentives: Tax breaks and concessions are used to attract investment into specialized sectors or developing regions.

Behavioral Modification: Taxes on harmful goods (e.g., tobacco, alcohol) can deter consumption, while tax incentives can encourage investments in eco-friendly or productive industries.

Ethics, resilience, and a service mindset are three foundational pillars of effective public leadership and professional excellence, especially relevant in public administration, taxation, and governance roles. An ethical officer without resilience may become discouraged.

A resilient officer without ethics may become authoritarian.

A service-oriented officer without ethics may become populist.

Balanced together, they create credible, stable, and citizen-centric administration.

Think of these three traits as the "internal operating system" for a high-impact life. Individually, they make you a better person; combined, they make you a formidable leader and teammate. Deepening your connection to these values requires moving past definitions and looking at your actual experiences. Reflecting on these isn't about "perfecting" yourself; it's about identifying your natural strengths and the moments where you have room to grow.

Ethics and values are the fundamental principles such as honesty, integrity, and respect that guide human behavior, decision-making, and social interaction. They are essential for building trust, ensuring accountability, fostering social harmony, and enabling long-term success in both personal life and professional environments by helping individuals distinguish right from wrong.

Ethics provide a framework for navigating complex dilemmas, allowing individuals to make choices that are fair, just, and responsible. Ethical behavior is crucial for establishing reputation, whether for individuals in relationships or organizations with stakeholders, fostering loyalty, and ensuring long-term success. Shared values (e.g., respect, empathy) hold communities together, preventing conflict and creating a more cohesive, peaceful society. In business and healthcare, ethical standards ensure accountability, patient welfare, and fair treatment, moving beyond legal requirements to maintain high standards of conduct. Adhering to strong moral values provides a sense of purpose and direction, leading to a more meaningful and principled life. Ethics and values act as the foundation for sustainable practices, ensuring that actions do not just provide short-term gains but are beneficial in the long run.

Without these guiding principles, a society risks chaos and a lack of trust in institutions and, on an individual level, a lack of personal purpose.

Ethics and values play an important role in enhancing human capital which in turn is crucial for any business and society. Ethics can give real and practical guidance. Being fair, honest and ethical is one the basic human needs. Every employee desires to be such himself and to work for an organization.

Negative attitudes towards ethics can cause devastating personal and social destruction.

Ethics isn't just about following the law; it's about doing the right thing when no one is looking and when the "right thing" is the harder choice. It is the foundation of trust. Ethics can be rigid or judgmental. Becomes a reliable guide for serving others fairly.

- **Integrity:** Consistency between your words and your actions.
- **Accountability:** Owning your mistakes rather than shifting blame.
- **Fairness**: Making decisions based on objective criteria rather than bias or personal gain.

The Litmus Test: Ask yourself, "If my decision was published on the front page of a newspaper tomorrow, would I be proud of it?"Ethics are tested most when there is a conflict between profit/convenience and principle.

The "Shadow" Moment: Think of a time you were tempted to take a shortcut. Did you take it? If so, what was the internal cost? If not, what gave you the strength to resist?

The Silent Witness: If a younger version of you or someone who looks up to you was watching your actions over the last week, what would they conclude about your character?

Your ethics should not change depending on who you are with, or are you the same person in the boardroom as you are at the dinner table.

Resilience is crucial in the workplace for maintaining productivity, mental well-being, and adaptability under pressure, which prevents burnout and fosters a positive, sustainable company culture. It enables employees to manage stress effectively, navigate rapid changes, and recover from setbacks, ultimately leading to higher engagement and consistent performance. Resilient employees can handle pressure without becoming overwhelmed, which lowers the risk of mental fatigue and burnout. Resilient individuals stay focused and motivated, ensuring consistent performance and goal achievement even during challenging times. In fast-paced industries, resilience helps teams adapt to organizational changes, restructuring, or technology. Resilience is the shock absorber. Resilience is often misunderstood as "toughing it out." In reality, it's the ability to navigate stress, adapt to change, and recover from setbacks without losing your drive. It's not about avoiding the storm; it's about knowing how to sail through it.

- **Emotional Regulation:** Staying calm under pressure so you can think clearly. It can be used for selfish or "villainous" ends. Ensures you stay ethical even when under extreme pressure.
- **Growth Mindset:** Viewing failures as data points and learning opportunities rather than personal indictments.
- **Persistence:** Maintaining your effort over the long haul, even when progress feels slow. Resilience is a muscle built through "resistance training."
- **The Recovery Rate:** Think about the last time a plan

fell apart. How long did it take you to move from "Why is this happening?" to "What do I do next?"

- **The Adaptation Lesson:** Identify a major setback from three years ago. What skills or perspectives do you have today only because that setback happened?
- **Energy Management:** When you are under high stress, do you isolate yourself, or do you reach out for support? Resilience is often a team sport.

A service-mindset in the workplace prioritizes customer satisfaction and colleague support, transforming routine tasks into relationship-building opportunities. It drives higher performance, fosters proactive problem-solving, enhances brand reputation, and strengthens team collaboration, ultimately shifting employee focus from transactional work to creating value and positive experiences. Cultivating this mindset ensures that work is not just a job, but a contribution to a larger, successful, and collaborative environment.

Employees who go above and beyond turn customer frustration into satisfaction, creating loyal advocates. A service mindset applied internally means supporting colleagues, which breaks down silos and builds trust.

Rather than just doing the minimum, individuals anticipate needs and address issues before they escalate. A service-oriented teamIncreased Productivity: A service-oriented team is more engaged and willing to help, boosting overall efficiency and organizational performance. A strong service culture sets a company apart, making it harder for competitors to match the quality of interaction.

Characteristics of a Service Mindset

- **Empathy:** Understanding and validating the user's or colleague's situation.
- **Proactivity:** Taking initiative to help without being asked.

- **Ownership:** Taking responsibility for finding a solution.

A service mindset shifts the focus from "What can I get?" to "How can I contribute?" This is the secret sauce of great customer service, effective leadership, and healthy relationships. It's about recognizing that your work exists to solve someone else's problem. Service can lead to burnout or being taken advantage of, is sustained by resilience and protected by ethical boundaries.

- **Empathy:** Actively seeking to understand the needs and pain points of others.
- **Proactivity:** Anticipating needs before they are voiced.
- **Humility:** Understanding that no task is "beneath you" if it helps the team or the mission succeed.

A service mindset is about the legacy you leave in your daily interactions.

- **The "Invisible" Task:** When was the last time you did something to help the team that you knew would never be credited to you? How did that feel?
- **Perspective Shifting:** In your most recent conflict, did you focus more on being right or on finding a solution that helped everyone involved?
- **The Value Chain:** If your role was removed tomorrow, who would feel the loss the most, and why? This identifies where your service is most impactful.

It is difficult to say that something is right or wrong. Since everything we see and do think and act upon takes place in a subjective, unreal, ever changing world. Morals and ethics, the two aspects of rights and wrongs, are really two different concepts. While morals change with passage of time, changing traditions and outlooks, ethics normally remain unchanged. Moral certainty is always a sign of cultural inferiority, said H L Mencken," The more uncivilized the man, the more he knows precisely what is right and what is wrong. All human progress, even in morals, has been the work of men who have doubted the current moral values, not of men who have whooped them up and tried to enforce them. The truly civilized man is always sceptical and tolerant, in this field as in all others".

Considering that the moral domain is not cast in stone, it is certainly not okay to stand or sit in judgement over whether something is morally right or wrong. Morals stem from behaviour based on personal beliefs, whereas ethics is something that the community and society agree upon as being right or wrong, and on the basis of which laws are formed and enforced. That is why when government agencies take it upon themselves to become moral police enforcing their ideas of behaviour, relationships or dress codes, it creates confusion and distasteful, even appalling to the civilized among us.

Framing Ethics, Resilience, and Service Mindset specifically for GST Officers requires aligning these values with tax administration realities, audits, investigations, adjudication, enforcement, and taxpayer interaction.

Ethics in GST Administration

GST officers exercise significant statutory powers under the Central Goods and Services Tax Act and related laws. Ethical conduct ensures these powers are used lawfully and fairly.

Core Ethical Responsibilities:

* **Integrity in Decision-Making**

- No misuse of summons, inspection, or arrest provisions.
- Avoiding coercive recovery without due process

- Ensuring evidence-based adjudication.

* Impartiality

- No discrimination between large corporations and MSMEs.
- Decisions based strictly on law and facts.

* **Transparency**

- Clear, reasoned orders.
- Speaking orders under Sections 73/74.
- Proper communication of deficiencies.

* **Confidentiality**

- Protection of business data and financial records.
- Responsible handling of sensitive taxpayer information.

* **Accountability**

- Readiness to justify actions before appellate forums and courts.
- Ethics builds credibility of GST as a modern, trust-based tax system.

Resilience in GST Role

GST administration operates in a dynamic and often high-pressure environment litigation, audit objections, system glitches, revenue targets, public scrutiny.

Areas Where Resilience is Critical:

* **Policy & System Changes**

- Frequent amendments.
- Portal challenges.
- Evolving jurisprudence.

* **Litigation Pressure**

- High-stakes cases.

- Court strictures.
- Audit paras and vigilance scrutiny.

* **Stakeholder Resistance**

- Non-cooperation during investigation.
- Aggressive representation by professionals. Revenue Expectations

  Balancing fairness with revenue safeguarding.

* **A resilient GST officer:**

- Remains calm under scrutiny.
- Learn from appellate reversals.
- Adapts to legal interpretations.
- Maintains morale despite external pressures.

Resilience ensures enforcement remains firm but not reactionary.

GST was designed as a "Good and Simple Tax" with technology and self-assessment at its core.

A service mindset transforms tax administration from fear-based to facilitation-based.

* **Service-Oriented Approach Includes:**

- Facilitating Voluntary Compliance
- Educating taxpayers.
- Clarifying doubts proactively.
- Conducting outreach programmes.

* **Respectful Interaction**

- Courteous behavior during summons or audit.
- Avoiding unnecessary harassment.
- Problem-Solving Orientation

Assisting in rectification rather than immediately penalizing.

Allowing opportunity of being heard.

* **Balancing Enforcement with Fairness**

- Strong against evasion.
- Supportive toward genuine mistakes.

Modern GST philosophy aligns with global best practices where tax officers are seen as compliance managers, not revenue collectors alone.

Integrated Framework for GST Officers

Dimension	Role in Administration	Outcome
Ethics	Ensures lawful and fair use of power	Prevents arbitrariness and misuse
Resilience	Maintains stability under pressure	Prevents burnout and reactive decisions
Service Mindset	Promotes citizen-centric approach	Encourages voluntary compliance and trust

* **Improves taxpayer relations**

During a GST audit:

Ethics ensures no arbitrary demand is raised.

Resilience helps handle aggressive rebuttals professionally. Service mindset allows guidance for future compliance rather than only imposing penalties. India's GST system is still evolving. Its long-term success depends not only on law and technology, but on the conduct of officers implementing it.

- Ethical strength ensures fairness.
- Resilience ensures continuity.
- Service mindset ensures trust.

Together, they transform tax administration into public service.

Practices like looking at the rising sun and chanting

the 'Om' come from ancient Indian traditions (especially Vedic and yogic systems). They are often associated with physical, mental, and spiritual benefits but it's important to separate scientifically supported effects from traditional beliefs.

1. **Effects of Staring at the Rising Sun (Sun Gazing)**

   Possible Benefits (when done safely)

- **Circadian rhythm regulation**

Early morning sunlight helps reset your biological clock, improving sleep quality and hormone balance.

- **Mood improvement**

Sunlight exposure boosts serotonin levels, reducing stress and mild depression.

- **Vitamin D synthesis (indirect)**

While eyes don't absorb vitamin D, early sunlight exposure encourages overall body exposure later in the day.

- **Eye relaxation (limited)**

Soft early sunlight may help relax eye muscles (only for a few seconds, not prolonged staring).

Important Caution. Directly staring at the sun even at sunrise can damage the retina (solar retinopathy) if done improperly or for too long.

Medical science does NOT recommend prolonged sun gazing.

- Safe approach:
- Keep it brief (a few seconds)
- Prefer looking slightly below/around the sun rather than directly at it
- Avoid once the sun becomes bright

2. **Effects of Chanting the Om'**

   Mental & Psychological Benefits

- **Improves concentration and focus**

Repetition of the mantra calms the mind and reduces distractions.

- **Reduces stress and anxiety**

Rhythmic chanting activates the parasympathetic nervous system (relaxation response).

- **Enhances emotional stability**

Regular practice promotes inner peace and clarity.

Spiritual & Traditional Beliefs

Traditionally believed to:

- **Purify the mind**

Increase wisdom and intellect

- **Align individual consciousness with universal energy**

Physical Effects

- **Improved breathing pattern**

Chanting involves controlled breathing, similar to pranayama.

- **Vibration effect**

Sound vibrations may stimulate areas of the brain and throat, promoting calmness.

Combined Practice (Sun + Mantra)

When done together (common in "Sandhya Vandana" practice):

- Creates a meditative state
- Enhances mind-body connection
- Builds discipline and routine
- Provides a sense of purpose and spiritual grounding

Balanced View

Aspect	Scientific Support	Traditional Belief
Sunlight exposure	Strong	Claimed beneficial
Mantra chanting	Moderate (mental health)	Strong
Spiritual awakening	Not measurable	Core belief

Practical Recommendation

- Do not stare directly at the sun for long
- Sit facing the sunrise with eyes gently closed or half-open
- Chant the Gayatri Mantra slowly with focus on breathing
- Practice for 5–10 minutes daily

***

Technology, Faceless Assessment, and the End of Discretion

Reform in the Indian Revenue Service did not arrive with a manifesto.It arrived with a dashboard.Screens replaced counters. Algorithms replaced discretion. Interfaces replaced faces. What vigilance could not always achieve through oversight, technology promised to accomplish through design.

The ambition was radical: remove the officer from the encounter, and corruption, coercion, and arbitrariness would wither.

This was the age of the faceless.

The Promise of Anonymity

Faceless assessment was sold as liberation for both taxpayer and officer. No more intimidating visits. No more whispered suggestions. No more proximity breeding pressure. Files would be allocated randomly. Officers would assess without knowing whom they were assessing. Decisions would be reviewed by anonymous peers.

In theory, this dismantled the marketplace of influence described in earlier chapters.

For many officers, the reform arrived with relief. The most vulnerable part of their authority the face-to-face encounter was gone. Pressure lost its point of entry.

For taxpayers, especially the compliant middle class, the promise was dignity without negotiation. It was, at first glance, an elegant solution.

The Disappearance of Context

What technology removes, however, is not only corruption. It removes context.

In the physical office, an officer saw hesitation, confusion, and intent. In the digital interface, behaviour is flattened into data fields and attachments. Algorithms do not recognise anxiety. Portals do not register sincerity.

A small mistake looks identical to a strategic omission. A confused pensioner appears indistinguishable from a sophisticated evader.

Discretion once allowed officers to compensate for this asymmetry. Faceless systems treat all deviations equally.

The officer now assesses without proximity, but also without intuition.

Discretion Rebranded, Not Eliminated

The reform promised the end of discretion. It delivered its redistribution.

Discretion did not vanish; it migrated. From individual officers to system designers. From field judgment to rule-making. From recorded reasoning to coded thresholds.

Algorithms decide what is flagged. Data analytics determine risk. Officers respond to prompts rather than patterns they discover themselves.

The question shifts: Who designs the discretion, and who audits it?

This discretion is harder to challenge. An officer can be cross-examined; an algorithm cannot explain itself easily.

The New Burden on Officers

Faceless assessment did not reduce workload. It rearranged it. Officers now handle unfamiliar cases from distant jurisdictions, with no local knowledge. Language barriers emerge. Industry context is missing. Time zones matter.

Communication becomes transactional. Clarifications are sought through templates. Responses arrive incomplete, late, or misunderstood. The officer's role shifts from investigator to verifier, from adjudicator to processor.

Many feel safer. Few feel satisfied.

Accountability Without Ownership

Anonymity protects, but it also dilutes responsibility. When multiple officers handle fragments of a case, ownership weakens. Decisions become collective but not accountable. Errors become systemic, not personal.Taxpayers struggle to identify who is responsible. Officers struggle to defend decisions they only partially made.

This diffusion of responsibility is efficient, but fragile. It reduces individual corruption, but increases institutional opacity.

The Officer as Data Point

In the new system, officers themselves are monitored. Dashboards track timelines. Metrics evaluate productivity. Alerts flag deviations. Performance is quantified relentlessly.

The officer becomes a data point within the same system he administers.

This symmetry is deliberate. Reformers argue that transparency must be mutual.

But quantification has limits. Not all good decisions are fast. Not all caution is inefficiency. The system rewards speed and volume more easily than judgment.

Taxpayer Experience: Relief and Alienation

For some taxpayers, faceless systems are a blessing. They remove intimidation. They reduce negotiation. They provide predictability.

For others, they are alienating. There is no one to explain confusion to. No one to sense misunderstanding.

Appeals become the only language.

Litigation rises not always because assessments are wrong, but because communication is insufficient.

Technology eliminates friction, but also empathy.

The Myth of Objectivity

Algorithms are perceived as neutral. They are not. They reflect the assumptions of their designers, the biases of data, the priorities of policy. What is flagged as risky reveals what the system fears.

Officers learn to work around these signals, sometimes amplifying them, sometimes compensating for them. The danger is complacency, trusting the system's objectivity without questioning its blind spots.

Resistance in a Digital Age

Resistance under faceless systems takes new forms. It is no longer about confrontation. It is about interpretation. About how strictly to apply system prompts. About when to escalate, and when to override.Officers with experience still exercise judgment but quietly, invisibly, within digital boundaries.

The courageous decision today is not to raid or resist, but to slow down a machine that prefers speed.

What Reform Reveals

Technology reveals something essential: that corruption was never only about contact. It was about concentration of power without accountability.

Faceless systems redistribute power, but they do not eliminate it. They trade discretion for design, visibility for scale.

The service becomes cleaner, but colder. Safer, but less humane.

Beyond the end of discretion it acknowledges a

transition. The Indian Revenue Service is moving from a relationship-based institution to a system-based one. From judgment exercised visibly to judgment embedded invisibly.

This transformation will outlast individual officers.

What remains uncertain is whether the system will retain the wisdom to recognise when discretion, human, imperfect, accountable is still necessary. Because even in a faceless regime, someone must decide. And where decisions exist, so does responsibility.

How AI May be used in better management of GST

In the context of the Indian Goods and Services Tax (GST) landscape in 2026, Artificial Intelligence (AI) has shifted from a futuristic concept to a core operational tool. It serves as a dual-force engine helping the GST Department catch evasion and helping Taxpayers (and professionals like CAs) maintain seamless compliance. To transition from using AI as a mere "fraud detector" to a fully integrated, proactive management system, India still needs to address several structural, legal, and technical "speed bumps." E-Invoicing Integration: Real-time AI analysis of e-invoices as they are generated to prevent errors at the source.

AI-Led Dispute Resolution: Using AI to predict the likely outcome of tax litigation based on historical judgments, helping businesses decide whether to settle or appeal.

Deep-Link Analysis: Identifying beneficial ownership and hidden connections between seemingly unrelated firms to prevent large-scale tax syndicates.

To fully operationalize an AI-driven GST administration, India needs reforms across law, data architecture, institutional design, and governance. While systems under GST Council, Central Board of Indirect Taxes and Customs, and the GSTN Portal have laid the foundation, the current setup is still fragmented, reactive, and partially digital. For AI-driven GST to truly work, India must move from:

"Digitization of old processes" to "Re-engineering GST around data and intelligence"

Despite the progress seen in the Union Budget 2026-27, the following reforms are crucial for a truly AI-driven GST model:

1. **Legal and Regulatory Reforms**

Algorithmic Transparency & Accountability: As the 2026 IT Rule Amendments mandate "provenance" for AI content, the GST department needs similar rules for its automated audit notices. Taxpayers need the right to know why an AI flagged them to prevent "Black Box" tax administration.

- **Clarification on "AI-Induced" Errors:** There is currently a legal gray area regarding liability if a taxpayer uses an AI tool (like an automated HSN classifier) that incorrectly files a return. Reforms must define whether the software provider or the taxpayer bears the penalty.
- **Statutory Recognition of Digital Evidence:** While AI can find "circular trading" patterns, the legal framework needs more robust provisions to accept AI-generated network maps as primary evidence in courts/tribunals without requiring exhaustive manual verification.

2. **Data Infrastructure & Integration**

Real-time "API-First" Mandate: Currently, data often moves in batches. To fully leverage AI, the government needs to mandate Universal API integration across all ERP systems. This would allow AI to catch errors at the moment of invoice generation rather than during month-end filing.

- **Cross-Departmental Data Lake:** AI is only as good

as its data. While "Project Insight" links Income Tax and GST, full integration with Customs (ICEGATE), MCA (Ministry of Corporate Affairs), and State Land Records is needed to create a 360-degree profile of a taxpayer.

- **Unified HSN Database:** There are still thousands of disputes over product classification (e.g., is a "paratha" a "roti"?). A centralized, AI-searchable database of all past Advance Rulings is needed so AI models can provide consistent tax rate advice.

3. **Structural & Administrative Reforms**

- **Transition from "Post-Facto" to "Real-Time" Audits:** The current system is reactive (audit happens after filing). The reform should move toward Continuous Assurance, where the GSTN's AI validates data before the return is finalized, reducing the need for future litigation.
- **Standardization of "Data Quality":** Many MSMEs still use disparate or manual accounting methods. For AI to work, there needs to be a push for Standard Audit File for Tax (SAF-T)—a global standard that makes business data readable by any AI regardless of the software used.

4. **The Human Element (Reskilling)**

- **GST Officers 2.0:** Tax officers need to be trained not just in law, but in Data Literacy. The reform is not just about the machine; it's about an Anomaly Score without falling into "automation bias" (assuming the machine is always right).
- **MSME Digital Subsidies:** Since high-end AI tools are expensive, the government may need to provide "GST-AI-as-a-Service" for small traders through the GSTN portal to ensure they aren't left behind by larger corporations with better tech.

The goal of these reforms is to move from a system of "Enforcement through Fear" to "Compliance by Design," where the AI makes it almost impossible to make a mistake in the first place.

***

Taxpayers, Trust, and the Crisis of Legitimacy

Most of us do not wake up thinking about tax. We think about milk prices, school fees, bus fares, mobile recharges, and whether the salary will last till month-end. Yet, quietly and constantly, tax walks with us through the day.

The road you travel on, the streetlight outside your home, the government hospital, the school where your child studies, all of them exist because citizens pay tax. Unlike charity, tax is not voluntary. But unlike extortion, it is meant to return to us in the form of public services.

GST (Goods and Services Tax) is one such tax that touches your life every single day. You may not see it clearly, but it is there in your grocery bill, your restaurant invoice, your movie ticket, and even your mobile phone plan. Understanding GST is not about becoming an accountant. It is about knowing how much you pay, why you pay, and when you should not be paying at all.

Of course, taxes do buy real things, defence, welfare programs, infra that take decades to reveal their full value. And returns on taxes cannot be reduced to personal perks simply because we pay taxes. The moral logic of taxation is collective, our taxes feed someone we will never meet, it may vaccinate a child whose name we will never know. That is not theft; that is the price of admission into society. And yet society also has standards and reciprocity. If the state wants more Indians to pay more taxes, it must show more competence. Indian roads are civic metaphor institutionalised corruption, they show us how perpetual repair is a form of governance. The roads have potholes problems, rather it enjoys an excavation culture. The real money does not come from building roads that last but from the endless cycle of re-tendering, redigging, relaying and rebilling and this is where our taxes go. And maybe that is why India has one of the highest net out flows of desi millionaires. Per projections from Henley and Partners private wealth migration report, India saw net out flows of about 5100 in 2023, 4300 in 2024, and 3500 in 2025 such millionaires. 35% of income tax is a first World tax grab for a fifth world return. So, the honest taxpayers observe non - delivery and then plots and exit, into cash, into creative accounting or into another passport. Democracy cannot run on compulsory citizens payments and optional government performance.

In India income re-distribution via taxes is not a freebie, it is the language of civilization. And yet it stings more than ever when we remember how few Indians actually pay taxes. In financial year 2023 24 only 6.68% of Indians filed an income tax return and PRS Legislature Research using CBDT data, shows that most files did not end up paying income tax in financial year 2022 - 23, 7.5 crore people filed returns, and 4.7 crore (63%) had zero tax liability. That means roughly 2.8 crores Indians had non zero Income tax liability, around 2% of the population. This small two percent club helps the lives of everyone else. However, all Indians pay taxes in the form of GST and other direct and indirect levies.

Further, the tax contribution by a citizen should be spent in providing welfare to them. Not clean air or water, not good roads or sanitation, not nice public hospitals. Sure too few Indians are tax payers but an incompetent State does not offer them fair returns either. The recent tragic death in Indore from contaminated water consumption clearly shows that it is not spent properly. Clean air can also be cut out of the equation, try breathing in Delhi today. IQ Air reports that in 2024 India's average PM2.5 was more than 10 times the WHO annual safety guidelines. A state unable to protect the air is turning every citizen into a patient. Now if you did fall sick in India, you could go to a state hospital to use the services your taxes paid for. But treatment in state run hospitals might feel far worse than sickness itself. As a result, and Niti Aayog's analysis confirms, about 60% of hospitalized cases are treated in the private sector even as government spending on public health rises. Citizens still pay private hospitals, private diagnostics and private insurance. As an Indian tax payer, the government stands at the front of the queue to yank your money and then makes you pay again, with your lungs, your guts and your peace of mind. Maybe the state gets away with this because the system is built so no one is responsible. The Government of India does grand announcements and ribbon cutting. States do implementation, then comes the clumsy explanation for why yet another newly constructed bridge collapsed. Cities are saddled with the mess we have to leave with, garbage, drains, potholes, and the famous tap water a la sewage. The 15th Finance Commission puts it plainly, our city governments are seriously underfunded and living on handouts while their own income shrinks. The government is adept at re- framing your life through the lens of its failures. At no point will the government simply admit that it gives you almost nothing back. But can we blame? Most of India does everything in its power to escape paying taxes. A large part of the economy is informal, incomes are uneven, seasonal under reported or hard to see. Enforcement is expensive, litigation is slow, so the state leans on the easiest levers: TDS for the complainant, GST for everyone, fuel duty for the resigned.

The Indian Revenue Service does not exist in isolation. Its authority rests on an invisible agreement between the State and its citizens, a belief that taxes are collected fairly, spent responsibly, and enforced without malice.

When that belief weakens, compliance becomes reluctant, enforcement becomes aggressive, and trust becomes a casualty.

This is the crisis of legitimacy.The Unequal Encounter For most citizens, interaction with the tax system is asymmetrical. The State arrives with forms, deadlines, and penalties. The citizen responds with incomplete understanding and quiet anxiety. Even in a faceless system, the imbalance remains. The portal speaks in notices; the citizen replies in explanations.

Few taxpayers question the necessity of taxes. Many question their fairness.They see visible waste, inconsistent enforcement, and narratives of impunity. They ask sometimes aloud, often privately why compliance feels punitive while evasion appears negotiable.

The officer, bound by law, inherits this distrust.

Compliance Without Conviction

India's tax base has expanded, but conviction has not kept pace. Many taxpayers comply because they must, not because they believe. Compliance becomes transactional an act of avoidance rather than participation.This distinction matters. Voluntary compliance relies on legitimacy. Coerced compliance relies on fear. The former sustains systems; the latter exhausts them.

The IRS operates increasingly in the second mode.

The Memory of Harassment

Institutional memory travels faster than institutional reform. Stories of harassment, real and exaggerated, persist long after procedures change. A raid from decades ago, a wrongful addition overturned on appeal, a business ruined by prolonged litigation these stories circulate widely.

For the taxpayer, one bad experience outweighs many silent correct ones.

Faceless assessment has reduced certain excesses, but it has not erased memory. Nor has it addressed the deeper grievance: the feeling of being presumed guilty.

Trust and the Burden of Proof

The law places the burden of proof unevenly.

Taxpayers must explain discrepancies. Officers must justify actions only when questioned. This asymmetry is legal, but it is also psychological.

Citizens experience it as suspicion institutionalised. Officers experience it as a necessity without presumption, evasion flourishes. Between these positions lies a fragile space where trust might grow.

The Middle Class Dilemma

The middle class occupies an uncomfortable place in this system. Too visible to evade, too dispersed to influence, too compliant to resist. It pays most reliably, complains most quietly, and receives least accommodation.

For this group, taxation becomes not a civic duty, but a test of endurance.Their frustration is rarely dramatic. It expresses itself in cynicism, disengagement, and private resentment.

This silent erosion of legitimacy is harder to detect than open protest.

Officers as Inheritors of Distrust

IRS officers do not create this distrust. They inherit it. Every new officer begins with a deficit not of authority, but of credibility. He must prove fairness before being trusted, even when acting lawfully. This is an exhausting position.

It requires patience in the face of suspicion, restraint in the face of provocation, and empathy without reciprocation.

Not all officers manage it. Not all taxpayers allow it.

One of the service's greatest failures has been

communication. Orders speak in law, not language. Notices inform without explaining. Portals notify without reassuring. Many disputes escalate not because positions are irreconcilable, but because explanations are absent. A reasoned decision poorly communicated feels arbitrary. A correct action without empathy feels hostile. Trust, once lost, cannot be rebuilt through efficiency alone.

Litigation as Dialogue

India's tax litigation backlog is often described as inefficiency. It is also dialogue by other means. When taxpayers feel unheard, they appeal. When officers feel challenged, they defend. Courts become translators between law and legitimacy.This is expensive, slow, and adversarial but it is also a measure of institutional failure.

Systems with high trust litigate less. Rising compliance numbers are celebrated.

But statistics cannot measure belief. A taxpayer may file returns punctually and still feel wronged. May pay taxes and still distrust the State.

Legitimacy is not visible in dashboards.

It reveals itself only when citizens choose honesty in situations where evasion would go unnoticed.

The Officer's Dilemma Revisited

Officers face an impossible demand: enforce rigorously without appearing hostile; be firm without seeming arbitrary; uphold law without embodying suspicion.

Faceless systems ease this burden procedurally, but not emotionally.

The officer becomes a functionary in a trust deficit he did not create and cannot resolve alone.

What Trust Requires

Trust requires consistency, transparency, and

explanation. It requires systems that admit error, officers who record reasoning, and institutions that correct excess visibly.

It requires time measured not in financial years, but in generations.Most of all, it requires humility, the State recognising that compliance is cooperation, not submission.

The Indian Revenue Service stands at a moment where enforcement is strong, technology sophisticated, and authority intact.

What remains fragile is legitimacy.

In the years ahead, the focus will shift again from systems to people, from reform to reflection and from crisis to possibility.

Because no tax system survives on power alone. It survives on belief.

***

Work, Family, and the Personal Cost of Power

Power is most visible in the office.Its cost is paid at home. The Indian Revenue Service confers authority early and sustains it long. Files move because an officer signs. Businesses pause because a notice arrives. Decisions made in air-conditioned rooms ripple through households the officer will never meet.

Yet when the office closes, power does not follow. What remains is fatigue, absence, and the quiet strain of a life lived under constant consequence.

The Geography of Separation

Few services disperse families as relentlessly.

Postings are frequent, transfers abrupt, tenures uncertain. Officers learn early not to unpack fully. Spouses postpone careers. Children change schools with the seasons.

The service calls this exposure. Families call it distance. Over time, relationships adjust not by choice, but by necessity. Birthdays are missed. Parents age elsewhere. Home becomes an idea rather than a place. This mobility is presented as professional neutrality. Its human cost is rarely calculated.

The Spouse as Silent Stakeholder

The officer's spouse bears power without authority. They absorb social scrutiny, manage domestic logistics, and navigate informal expectations often without guidance or recognition. In many cases, they sacrifice independent careers to sustain stability the service cannot provide.Their lives are shaped by postings they do not choose and reputations they cannot control. They learn discretion without training. Resilience without acknowledgment.

The service counts one officer. It relies on two.

Children of the Service

Children adapt quickly and remember quietly.

They learn not to ask when the next move will come. They avoid attachments that will be broken. They internalise uncertainty as normal.

Some thrive. Others resent.

The service appears to children not as prestige, but as interruption. Authority in office does not translate to availability at home.

Power, to a child, is measured in presence.

The Weight of Reputation

An officer's identity rarely remains private.

Neighbours speculate. Relatives inquire. Friends assume access. The uniform of authority is worn even when invisible.

Success invites envy. Failure invites judgement. Neutrality invites suspicion.

The family inherits these projections. They are praised without achievement and blamed without fault.

Privacy becomes a luxury.

The Loneliness of Command

Leadership isolates.

Officers cannot confide freely. Subordinates listen strategically. Peers compete quietly. Superiors evaluate constantly.

The space for unguarded conversation shrinks.

At home, the officer struggles to shed command.

Authority lingers in tone, impatience, and expectation. Family members become witnesses to stress they cannot relieve.

Power without companionship is heavy.

Ethics at the Dinner Table

Decisions made at work do not end there.

An assessment order, a raid, a vigilance inquiry these follow the officer home in thought if not in speech. Silence becomes a coping mechanism. Families sense tension without explanation. They learn not to ask too much.

The service trains officers in law, not in emotional containment.

For women officers, the cost is multiplied.

They negotiate authority in male-dominated spaces while managing expectations at home that have not evolved at the same pace. Transfers disrupt fragile support systems. Safety, schooling, and social scrutiny intensify stress. The service celebrates their presence. The system still tests their endurance.

Progress exists, but unevenly.

The Myth of Prestige From outside, the service appears prestigious. From inside, prestige is conditional. Officers discover that respect depends on position, not principle. On power held, not character shown. A posting defines worth more than years of integrity.This realization is sobering.At home, family members encounter admiration that feels hollow, because they know the cost behind it.

Burnout Without Vocabulary

The service does not recognise burnout.

It recognises delay, deviation, and decline. Emotional exhaustion is interpreted as inefficiency. Detachment as disinterest.

Officers rarely name their fatigue. There is no safe language for vulnerability.

Family becomes the only refuge and sometimes, the unintended casualty.

Despite the cost, families provide something the service cannot: perspective.

A child's indifference to rank, a spouse's insistence on presence, an aging parent's needs these puncture institutional illusion.

They remind the officer that authority is temporary, but relationships are not.

Many officers survive the service because their families anchor them to life beyond files.

The Quiet Reckoning

Near retirement, officers reflect.

They measure careers not in positions held, but in moments missed. They ask whether the cost was justified. Some answer yes. Others are unsure. The service records service length. Families remember absence length.

This reckoning is personal, irreversible, and largely unspoken.

The Indian Revenue Service grants authority generously and demands sacrifice quietly.

Those who endure do so not because the cost is small, but because meaning however defined compensates.

Because in the end, power is temporary.

What endures is what it costs and what it leaves intact.

***

www.ingramcontent.com/pod-product-compliance
Lightning Source LLC
LaVergne TN
LVHW100145061126
851857LV00010B/247
9789362105158